REQUIEM FOR A NUN

WILLIAM FAULKNER

REQUIEM
for a NUN

RANDOM HOUSE   **NEW YORK**

CONTENTS

REQUIEM FOR A NUN

ACT ONE

THE COURTHOUSE (A Name for the City)

The courthouse is less old than the town, which began somewhere under the turn of the century as a Chickasaw Agency trading-post and so continued for almost thirty years before it discovered, not that it lacked a depository for its records and certainly not that it needed one, but that only by creating or anyway decreeing one, could it cope with a situation which otherwise was going to cost somebody money;

The settlement had the records; even the simple dispossession of Indians begot in time a minuscule of archive, let alone the normal litter of man's ramshackle confederation against environment—that time and that wilderness—in this case, a meagre, fading, dogeared, uncorrelated, at times illiterate sheaf of land grants and patents and transfers and deeds, and tax- and militia-rolls, and bills of sale for slaves, and counting-house lists of spurious currency and exchange rates, and liens and mortgages, and listed rewards for escaped or stolen Negroes and other livestock, and diary-like annotations of births and marriages and deaths and public hangings and land-auctions, accumulating slowly for those three decades in a sort of iron pirate's chest in the back room of the postoffice-tradingpost-store, until that day thirty years later when, because of a jailbreak compounded by an ancient monster iron padlock transported a thousand

miles by horseback from Carolina, the box was removed
to a small new leanto room like a wood- or tool-shed built
two days ago against one outside wall of the morticed-
log mud-chinked shake-down jail; and thus was born
the Yoknapatawpha County courthouse: by simple fortuity, not only less old than even the jail, but come into
existence at all by chance and accident: the box containing the documents not moved from any place, but
simply to one; removed from the trading-post back room
not for any reason inherent in either the back room or
the box, but on the contrary: which—the box—was not
only in nobody's way in the back room, it was even
missed when gone since it had served as another seat or
stool among the powder- and whisky-kegs and firkins of
salt and lard about the stove on winter nights; and was
moved at all for the simple reason that suddenly the
settlement (overnight it would become a town without
having been a village; one day in about a hundred
years it would wake frantically from its communal slumber into a rash of Rotary and Lion Clubs and Chambers
of Commerce and City Beautifuls: a furious beating of
hollow drums toward nowhere, but merely to sound
louder than the next little human clotting to its north
or south or east or west, dubbing itself city as Napoleon
dubbed himself emperor and defending the expedient
by padding its census rolls—a fever, a delirium in which
it would confound forever seething with motion and motion with progress. But that was a hundred years away
yet; now it was frontier, the men and women pioneers,

tough, simple, and durable, seeking money or adventure
or freedom or simple escape, and not too particular how
they did it.) discovered itself faced not so much with a
problem which had to be solved, as a Damocles sword of
dilemma from which it had to save itself;

Even the jailbreak was fortuity: a gang—three or four
—of Natchez Trace bandits (twenty-five years later legend would begin to affirm, and a hundred years later
would still be at it, that two of the bandits were the
Harpes themselves, Big Harpe anyway, since the cir-
cumstances, the method of the breakout left behind like
a smell, an odor, a kind of gargantuan and bizarre play-
fulness at once humorous and terrifying, as if the settlement had fallen, blundered, into the notice or range of
an idle and whimsical giant. Which—that they were the
Harpes—was impossible, since the Harpes and even the
last of Mason's ruffians were dead or scattered by this
time, and the robbers would have had to belong to John
Murrel's organization—if they needed to belong to any
at all other than the simple fraternity of rapine.) captured by chance by an incidental band of civilian more-
or-less militia and brought in to the Jefferson jail because
it was the nearest one, the militia band being part of a
general muster at Jefferson two days before for a Fourth-
of-July barbecue, which by the second day had been
refined by hardy elimination into one drunken brawling
which rendered even the hardiest survivors vulnerable
enough to be ejected from the settlement by the civilian

residents, the band which was to make the capture having
been carried, still comatose, in one of the evicting wagons to a swamp four miles from Jefferson known as
Hurricane Bottoms, where they made camp to regain
their strength or at least their legs, and where that night
the four—or three—bandits, on the way across country
to their hideout from their last exploit on the Trace,
stumbled onto the campfire. And here report divided;
some said that the sergeant in command of the militia
recognised one of the bandits as a deserter from his
corps, others said that one of the bandits recognised in
the sergeant a former follower of his, the bandit's, trade.
Anyway, on the fourth morning all of them, captors and
prisoners, returned to Jefferson in a group, some said in
confederation now seeking more drink, others said that
the captors brought their prizes back to the settlement in
revenge for having been evicted from it. Because these
were frontier, pioneer times, when personal liberty and
freedom were almost a physical condition like fire or
flood, and no community was going to interfere with anyone's morals as long as the amoralist practised somewhere else, and so Jefferson, being neither on the Trace
nor the River but lying about midway between, naturally
wanted no part of the underworld of either;

But they had some of it now, taken as it were by sur-
prise, unawares, without warning to prepare and fend
off. They put the bandits into the log-and-mudchinking
jail, which until now had had no lock at all since its

clients so far had been amateurs—local brawlers and drunkards and runaway slaves—for whom a single heavy wooden beam in slots across the outside of the door like on a corncrib, had sufficed. But they had now what might be four—three—Dillingers or Jesse Jameses of the time, with rewards on their heads. So they locked the jail; they bored an auger hole through the door and another through the jamb and passed a length of heavy chain through the holes and sent a messenger on the run across to the postoffice-store to fetch the ancient Carolina lock from the last Nashville mail-pouch—the iron monster weighing almost fifteen pounds, with a key almost as long as a bayonet, not just the only lock in that part of the country, but the oldest lock in that cranny of the United States, brought there by one of the three men who were what was to be Yoknapatawpha County's co-eval pioneers and settlers, leaving in it the three oldest names—Alexander Holston, who came as half groom and half bodyguard to Doctor Samuel Habersham, and half nurse and half tutor to the doctor's eight-year-old motherless son, the three of them riding horseback across Tennessee from the Cumberland Gap along with Louis Grenier, the Huguenot younger son who brought the first slaves into the country and was granted the first big land patent and so became the first cotton planter; while Doctor Habersham, with his worn black bag of pills and knives and his brawny taciturn bodyguard and his half orphan child, became the settlement itself (for a time, before it was named, the settlement was known as Doctor

Habersham's, then Habersham's, then simply Habersham; a hundred years later, during a schism between two ladies' clubs over the naming of the streets in order to get free mail delivery, a movement was started, first, to change the name back to Habersham; then, failing that, to divide the town in two and call one half of it Habersham after the old pioneer doctor and founder)— friend of old Issetibbeha, the Chickasaw chief (the motherless Habersham boy, now a man of twenty-five, married one of Issetibbeha's grand-daughters and in the thirties emigrated to Oklahoma with his wife's dispossessed people), first unofficial, then official Chickasaw agent until he resigned in a letter of furious denunciation addressed to the President of the United States himself; and—his charge and pupil a man now—Alexander Holston became the settlement's first publican, establishing the tavern still known as the Holston House, the original log walls and puncheon floors and hand-morticed joints of which are still buried somewhere beneath the modern pressed glass and brick veneer and neon tubes. The lock was his;

Fifteen pounds of useless iron lugged a thousand miles through a desert of precipice and swamp, of flood and drouth and wild beasts and wild Indians and wilder white men, displacing that fifteen pounds better given to food or seed to plant food or even powder to defend with, to become a fixture, a kind of landmark, in the bar of a wilderness ordinary, locking and securing nothing, be-

cause there was nothing behind the heavy bars and
shutters needing further locking and securing; not even
a paper weight because the only papers in the Holston
House were the twisted spills in an old powder horn
above the mantel for lighting tobacco; always a little in
the way, since it had constantly to be moved: from bar
to shelf to mantel then back to bar again until they
finally thought about putting it on the bi-monthly mail-
pouch; familiar, known, presently the oldest unchanged
thing in the settlement, older than the people since Issetibbeha and Doctor Habersham were dead, and Alexander
Holston was an old man crippled with arthritis, and
Louis Grenier had a settlement of his own on his vast
plantation, half of which was not even in Yoknapatawpha
County, and the settlement rarely saw him; older than
the town, since there were new names in it now even when
the old blood ran in them—Sartoris and Stevens, Compson and McCaslin and Sutpen and Coldfield—and you
no longer shot a bear or deer or wild turkey simply by
standing for a while in your kitchen door, not to mention
the pouch of mail—letters and even newspapers—which
came from Nashville every two weeks by a special rider
who did nothing else and was paid a salary for it by the
Federal Government; and that was the second phase of
the monster Carolina lock's transubstantiation into the
Yoknapatawpha County courthouse;

The pouch didn't always reach the settlement every
two weeks, nor even always every month. But sooner or

later it did, and everybody knew it would, because it—
the cowhide saddlebag not even large enough to hold a
full change of clothing, containing three or four letters
and half that many badly-printed one- and two-sheet
newspapers already three or four months out of date and
usually half and sometimes wholly misinformed or in-
correct to begin with—was the United States, the power
and the will to liberty, owning liegence to no man, bringing even into that still almost pathless wilderness the
thin peremptory voice of the nation which had wrenched
its freedom from one of the most powerful peoples on
earth and then again within the same lifespan success-
fully defended it; so peremptory and audible that the
man who carried the pouch on the galloping horse didn't
even carry any arms except a tin horn, traversing month
after month, blatantly, flagrantly, almost contemptu-
ously, a region where for no more than the boots on his
feet, men would murder a traveller and gut him like a
bear or deer or fish and fill the cavity with rocks and sink
the evidence in the nearest water; not even deigning to
pass quietly where other men, even though armed and in
parties, tried to move secretly or at least without uproar,
but instead announcing his solitary advent as far ahead
of himself as the ring of the horn would carry. So it was
not long before Alexander Holston's lock had moved to
the mail-pouch. Not that the pouch needed one, having
come already the three hundred miles from Nashville
without a lock. (It had been projected at first that the
lock remain on the pouch constantly. That is, not just

while the pouch was in the settlement, but while it was
on the horse between Nashville and the settlement too.
The rider refused, succinctly, in three words, one of
which was printable. His reason was the lock's weight.
They pointed out to him that this would not hold water,
since not only—the rider was a frail irascible little man
weighing less than a hundred pounds—would the fifteen
pounds of lock even then fail to bring his weight up to
that of a normal adult male, the added weight of the lock
would merely match that of the pistols which his employer, the United States Government, believed he carried and even paid him for having done so, the rider's
reply to this being succinct too though not so glib: that
the lock weighed fifteen pounds either at the back door
of the store in the settlement, or at that of the postoffice
in Nashville. But since Nashville and the settlement were
three hundred miles apart, by the time the horse had
carried it from one to the other, the lock weighed fifteen
pounds to the mile times three hundred miles, or forty-
five hundred pounds. Which was manifest nonsense, a
physical impossibility either in lock or horse. Yet indu-
bitably fifteen pounds times three hundred miles was
forty-five hundred something, either pounds or miles—
especially as while they were still trying to unravel it,
the rider repeated his first three succinct—two unprint-
able—words.) So less than ever would the pouch need
a lock in the back room of the trading-post, surrounded
and enclosed once more by civilization, where its very
intactness, its presence to receive a lock, proved its lack

of that need during the three hundred miles of rapine-haunted Trace; needing a lock as little as it was equipped to receive one, since it had been necessary to slit the leather with a knife just under each jaw of the opening and insert the lock's iron mandible through the two slits and clash it home, so that any other hand with a similar knife could have cut the whole lock from the pouch as easily as it had been clasped onto it. So the old lock was not even a symbol of security: it was a gesture of salutation, of free men to free men, of civilization to civilization across not just the three hundred miles of wilderness to Nashville, but the fifteen hundred to Washington: of respect without servility, allegiance without abasement to the government which they had helped to found and had accepted with pride but still as free men, still free to withdraw from it at any moment when the two of them found themselves no longer compatible, the old lock meeting the pouch each time on its arrival, to clasp it in iron and inviolable symbolism, while old Alec Holston, childless bachelor, grew a little older and grayer, a little more arthritic in flesh and temper too, a little stiffer and more rigid in bone and pride too, since the lock was still his, he had merely lent it, and so in a sense he was the grandfather in the settlement of the inviolability not just of government mail, but of a free government of free men too, so long as the government remembered to let men live free, not under it but beside it;

That was the lock; they put it on the jail. They did it quickly, not even waiting until a messenger could have got back from the Holston House with old Alec's permission to remove it from the mail-pouch or use it for the new purpose. Not that he would have objected on principle nor refused his permission except by simple instinct; that is, he would probably have been the first to suggest the lock if he had known in time or thought of it first, but he would have refused at once if he thought the thing was contemplated without consulting him. Which everybody in the settlement knew, though this was not at all why they didn't wait for the messenger. In fact, no messenger had ever been sent to old Alec; they didn't have time to send one, let alone wait until he got back; they didn't want the lock to keep the bandits in, since (as was later proved) the old lock would have been no more obstacle for the bandits to pass than the customary wooden bar; they didn't need the lock to protect the settlement from the bandits, but to protect the bandits from the settlement. Because the prisoners had barely reached the settlement when it developed that there was a faction bent on lynching them at once, out of hand, without preliminary—a small but determined gang which tried to wrest the prisoners from their captors while the militia was still trying to find someone to surrender them to, and would have succeeded except for a man named Compson, who had come to the settlement a few years ago with a race-horse, which he swapped to Ikkemotubbe, Issetibbeha's successor in the chiefship, for a square mile of what was to be the most valuable land in the future town of Jefferson, who, legend said, drew a pistol and held the ravishers at bay until the bandits could be got into the jail and the auger holes bored and someone sent to fetch old Alec Holston's lock. Because there were indeed new names and faces too in the settlement now—faces so new as to have (to the older residents) no discernible antecedents other than mammalinity, nor past other than the simple years which had scored them; and names so new as to have no discernible (nor discoverable either) antecedents or past at all, as though they had been invented yesterday, report dividing again: to the effect that there were more people in the settlement that day than the militia sergeant whom one or all of the bandits might recognise;

So Compson locked the jail, and a courier with the two best horses in the settlement—one to ride and one to lead —cut through the woods to the Trace to ride the hundred-odd miles to Natchez with news of the capture and authority to dicker for the reward; and that evening in the Holston House kitchen was held the settlement's first municipal meeting, prototype not only of the town council after the settlement would be a town, but of the Chamber of Commerce when it would begin to proclaim itself a city, with Compson presiding, not old Alec, who was quite old now, grim, taciturn, sitting even on a hot July night before a smoldering log in his vast chimney, his back even turned to the table (he was not interested in the deliberation; the prisoners were his already since his lock held them; whatever the conference decided would have to be submitted to him for ratification anyway before anyone could touch his lock to open it) around which the progenitors of the Jefferson city fathers sat in what was almost a council of war, not only discussing the collecting of the reward, but the keeping and defending it. Because there were two factions of opposition now: not only the lynching party, but the militia band too, who now claimed that as prizes the prisoners still belonged to their original captors; that they—the militia —had merely surrendered the prisoners' custody but had relinquished nothing of any reward: on the prospect of which, the militia band had got more whiskey from the trading-post store and had built a tremendous bonfire in front of the jail, around which they and the lynching party had now confederated in a wassail or conference of their own. Or so they thought. Because the truth was that Compson, in the name of a crisis in the public peace and welfare, had made a formal demand on the professional bag of Doctor Peabody, old Doctor Habersham's successor, and the three of them—Compson, Peabody, and the post trader (his name was Ratcliffe; a hundred years later it would still exist in the county, but by that time it had passed through two inheritors who had dispensed with the eye in the transmission of words, using only the ear, so that by the time the fourth one had been compelled by simple necessity to learn to write it again, it had lost the 'c' and the final 'fe' too) added the laudanum to the keg of whiskey and sent it as a gift from the settlement to the astonished militia sergeant, and returned to the Holston House kitchen to wait until the last of the uproar died; then the law-and-order party made a rapid sortie and gathered up all the comatose opposition, lynchers and captors too, and dumped them all into the jail with the prisoners and locked the door again and went home to bed—until the next morning, when the first arrivals were met by a scene resembling an outdoor stage setting: which was how the legend of the mad Harpes started: a thing not just fantastical but incomprehensible, not just whimsical but a little terrifying (though at least it was bloodless, which would have contented neither Harpe): not just the lock gone from the door nor even just the door gone from the jail, but the entire wall gone, the mud-chinked axe-morticed logs unjointed neatly and quietly in the darkness and stacked as neatly to one side, leaving the jail open to the world like a stage on which the late insurgents still lay sprawled and various in deathlike slumber, the whole settlement gathered now to watch Compson trying to kick at least one of them awake, until one of the Holston slaves—the cook's husband, the waiter-groom-hostler—ran into the crowd shouting, 'Whar de lock, whar de lock, ole Boss say whar de lock.'

It was gone (as were three horses belonging to three of the lynching faction). They couldn't even find the heavy door and the chain, and at first they were almost betrayed into believing that the bandits had had to take the door in order to steal the chain and lock, catching themselves back from the very brink of this wanton accusation of rationality. But the lock was gone; nor did it

take the settlement long to realise that it was not the
escaped bandits and the aborted reward, but the lock,
and not a simple situation which faced them, but a problem which threatened, the slave departing back to the
Holston House at a dead run and then reappearing at the
dead run almost before the door, the walls, had had time
to hide him, engulf and then eject him again, darting
through the crowd and up to Compson himself now, saying, 'Ole Boss say fetch de lock'—not send the lock, but
bring the lock. So Compson and his lieutenants (and this
was where the mail rider began to appear, or rather, to
emerge—the fragile wisp of a man ageless, hairless and
toothless, who looked too frail even to approach a horse,
let alone ride one six hundred miles every two weeks, yet
who did so, and not only that but had wind enough left
not only to announce and precede but even follow his
passing with the jeering musical triumph of the horn:—
a contempt for possible—probable—despoilers matched
only by that for the official dross of which he might be
despoiled, and which agreed to remain in civilised
bounds only so long as the despoilers had the taste to refrain)—repaired to the kitchen where old Alec still sat
before his smoldering log, his back still to the room, and
still not turning it this time either. And that was all. He
ordered the immediate return of his lock. It was not even
an ultimatum, it was a simple instruction, a decree, impersonal, the mail rider now well into the fringe of the
group, saying nothing and missing nothing, like a weightless desiccated or fossil bird, not a vulture of course nor

even quite a hawk, but say a pterodactyl chick arrested just out of the egg ten glaciers ago and so old in simple infancy as to be the worn and weary ancestor of all subsequent life. They pointed out to old Alec that the only reason the lock could be missing was that the bandits had not had time or been able to cut it out of the door, and that even three fleeing madmen on stolen horses would not carry a six-foot oak door very far, and that a party of Ikkemotubbe's young men were even now trailing the horses westward toward the River and that without doubt the lock would be found at any moment, probably under the first bush at the edge of the settlement: knowing better, knowing that there was no limit to the fantastic and the terrifying and the bizarre, of which the men were capable who already, just to escape from a log jail, had quietly removed one entire wall and stacked it in neat piecemeal at the roadside, and that they nor old Alec neither would ever see his lock again;

Nor did they; the rest of that afternoon and all the next day too, while old Alec still smoked his pipe in front of his smoldering log, the settlement's sheepish and raging elders hunted for it, with (by now: the next afternoon) Ikkemotubbe's Chickasaws helping too, or anyway present, watching: the wild men, the wilderness's tameless evictant children looking only the more wild and homeless for the white man's denim and butternut and felt and straw which they wore, standing or squatting or following, grave, attentive and interested, while the white men sweated and cursed among the bordering thickets of their punily-clawed foothold; and always the rider, Pettigrew, ubiquitous, everywhere, not helping search himself and never in anyone's way, but always present, inscrutable, saturnine, missing nothing: until at last toward sundown Compson crashed savagely out of the last bramble-brake and flung the sweat from his face with a full-armed sweep sufficient to repudiate a throne, and said,

'All right, god damn it, we'll pay him for it.' Because they had already considered that last gambit; they had already realised its seriousness from the very fact that Peabody had tried to make a joke about it which everyone knew that even Peabody did not think humorous:

'Yes—and quick too, before he has time to advise with Pettigrew and price it by the pound.'

'By the pound?' Compson said.

'Pettigrew just weighed it by the three hundred miles from Nashville. Old Alec might start from Carolina. That's fifteen thousand pounds.'

'Oh,' Compson said. So he blew in his men by means of a foxhorn which one of the Indians wore on a thong around his neck, though even then they paused for one last quick conference; again it was Peabody who stopped them.

'Who'll pay for it?' he said. 'It would be just like him to want a dollar a pound for it, even if by Pettigrew's scale he had found it in the ashes of his fireplace.'

They—Compson anyway—had probably already thought of that; that, as much as Pettigrew's presence, was probably why he was trying to rush them into old Alec's presence with the offer so quickly that none would have the face to renege on a pro-rata share. But Peabody had torn it now. Compson looked about at them, sweating, grimly enraged.

'That means Peabody will probably pay one dollar,' he said. 'Who pays the other fourteen? Me?' Then Ratcliffe, the trader, the store's proprietor, solved it—a solution so simple, so limitless in retroact, that they didn't even wonder why nobody had thought of it before; which not only solved the problem but abolished it; and not just that one, but all problems, from now on into perpetuity, opening to their vision like the rending of a veil, like a glorious prophecy, the vast splendid limitless panorama of America: that land of boundless opportunity, that bourne, created not by nor of the people, but for the people, as was the heavenly manna of old, with no return demand on man save the chewing and swallowing since out of its own matchless Allgood it would create produce train support and perpetuate a race of laborers dedicated to the single purpose of picking the manna up and putting it into his lax hand or even between his jaws—illimitable, vast, without beginning or end, not even a trade or a craft but a beneficence as are sunlight and rain and air, inalienable and immutable.

'Put it on the Book,' Ratcliffe said—the Book: not a ledger, but *the* ledger, since it was probably the only thing of its kind between Nashville and Natchez, unless there might happen to be a similar one a few miles south at the first Choctaw agency at Yalo Busha—a ruled, paper-backed copybook such as might have come out of a schoolroom, in which accrued, with the United States as debtor, in Mohataha's name (the Chickasaw matriarch, Ikkemotubbe's mother and old Issetibbeha's sister, who—she could write her name, or anyway make something with a pen or pencil which was agreed to be, or at least accepted to be, a valid signature—signed all the conveyances as her son's kingdom passed to the white people, regularising it in law anyway) the crawling tedious list of calico and gunpowder, whiskey and salt and snuff and denim pants and osseous candy drawn from Ratcliffe's shelves by her descendants and subjects and Negro slaves. That was all the settlement had to do: add the lock to the list, the account. It wouldn't even matter at what price they entered it. They could have priced it on Pettigrew's scale of fifteen pounds times the distance not just to Carolina but to Washington itself, and nobody would ever notice it probably; they could have charged the United States with seventeen thousand five hundred dollars' worth of the fossilised and indestructible candy, and none would ever read the entry. So it was solved, done, finished, ended. They didn't even have to discuss it. They didn't even think about it any more, unless perhaps here and there to marvel (a little speculatively probably) at their own moderation, since they wanted nothing—least of all, to

escape any just blame—but a fair and decent adjust-
ment of the lock. They went back to where old Alec still
sat with his pipe in front of his dim hearth. Only they
had overestimated him; he didn't want any money at
all, he wanted his lock. Whereupon what little remained
of Compson's patience went too.

'Your lock's gone,' he told old Alec harshly.
'You'll take fifteen dollars for it,' he said, his voice already fading, because even that rage could recognise
impasse when it saw it. Nevertheless, the rage, the impotence, the sweating, the *too much*—whatever it was—
forced the voice on for one word more: 'Or—' before
it stopped for good and allowed Peabody to fill the gap:

'Or else?' Peabody said, and not to old Alec,
but to Compson. 'Or else what?' Then Ratcliffe saved
that too.

'Wait,' he said. 'Uncle Alec's going to take fifty
dollars for his lock. A guarantee of fifty dollars. He'll
give us the name of the blacksmith back in Cal'lina that
made it for him, and we'll send back there and have a
new one made. Going and coming and all'll cost about
fifty dollars. We'll give Uncle Alec the fifty dollars to
hold as a guarantee. Then when the new lock comes, he'll
give us back the money. All right, Uncle Alec?' And
that could have been all of it. It probably would have
been, except for Pettigrew. It was not that they had forgotten him, nor even assimilated him. They had simply
sealed—healed him off (so they thought)—him into
their civic crisis as the desperate and defenseless oyster

immobilises its atom of inevictable grit. Nobody had seen him move yet he now stood in the center of them where Compson and Ratcliffe and Peabody faced old Alec in the chair. You might have said that he had oozed there, except for that adamantine quality which might (in emergency) become invisible but never insubstantial and never in this world fluid; he spoke in a voice bland, reasonable and impersonal, then stood there being looked at, frail and child-sized, impermeable as diamond and manifest with portent, bringing into that backwoods room a thousand miles deep in pathless wilderness, the whole vast incalculable weight of federality, not just representing the government nor even himself just the government; for that moment at least, he was the United States.

'Uncle Alec hasn't lost any lock,' he said. 'That was Uncle Sam.'

After a moment someone said, 'What?'

'That's right,' Pettigrew said. 'Whoever put that lock of Holston's on that mail bag either made a voluntary gift to the United States, and the same law covers the United States Government that covers minor children: you can give something to them, but you can't take it back, or he or they done something else.'

They looked at him. Again after a while somebody said something; it was Ratcliffe. 'What else?' Ratcliffe said. Pettigrew answered, still bland, impersonal, heatless and glib: 'Committed a violation of act of Congress as especially made and provided for the defacement of government property, penalty of five thousand dollars or not less than one year in a Federal jail or both. For whoever cut them two slits in the bag to put the lock in, act of Congress as especially made and provided for the injury or destruction of government property, penalty of ten thousand dollars or not less than five years in a Federal jail or both.' He did not move even yet; he simply spoke directly to old Alec: 'I reckon you're going to have supper here same as usual sooner or later or more or less.'

'Wait,' Ratcliffe said. He turned to Compson. 'Is that true?'

'What the hell difference does it make whether it's true or not?' Compson said. 'What do you think he's going to do as soon as he gets to Nashville?' He said violently to Pettigrew: 'You were supposed to leave for Nashville yesterday. What were you hanging around here for?'

'Nothing to go to Nashville for,' Pettigrew said. 'You dont want any mail. You aint got anything to lock it up with.'

'So we aint,' Ratcliffe said. 'So we'll let the United States find the United States' lock.' This time Pettigrew looked at no one. He wasn't even speaking to anyone, any more than old Alec had been when he decreed the return of his lock:

'Act of Congress as made and provided for the unauthorised removal and or use or willful or felonious use or misuse or loss of government property, penalty the value of the article plus five hundred to ten thousand dollars or thirty days to twenty years in a Federal jail or both. They may even make a new one when they read where you have charged a postoffice department lock to the Bureau of Indian Affairs.' He moved; now he was speaking to old Alec again: 'I'm going out to my horse. When this meeting is over and you get back to cooking, you can send your nigger for me.'

Then he was gone. After a while Ratcliffe said, 'What do you reckon he aims to get out of this? A reward?' But that was wrong; they all knew better than that.

'He's already getting what he wants,' Compson said, and cursed again. 'Confusion. Just damned confusion.' But that was wrong too; they all knew that too, though it was Peabody who said it:

'No. Not confusion. A man who will ride six hundred miles through this country every two weeks, with nothing for protection but a foxhorn, aint really interested in confusion any more than he is in money.' So they didn't know yet what was in Pettigrew's mind. But they knew what he would do. That is, they knew that they did not know at all, either what he would do, or how, or when, and that there was nothing whatever that they could do about it until they discovered why. And they saw now that they had no possible means to discover that; they realised now that they had known him for three years now, during which, fragile and inviolable and undeviable and preceded for a mile or more by the strong sweet ringing of the horn, on his strong and tireless horse he would complete the bi-monthly trip from Nashville to the settlement and for the next three or four days would live among them, yet that they knew nothing whatever about him, and even now knew only that they dared not, simply dared not, take any chance, sitting for a while longer in the darkening room while old Alec still smoked, his back still squarely turned to them and their quandary too; then dispersing to their own cabins for the evening meal—with what appetite they could bring to it, since presently they had drifted back through the summer darkness when by ordinary they would have been already in bed, to the back room of Ratcliffe's store now, to sit again while Ratcliffe recapitulated in his mixture of bewilderment and alarm (and something else which they recognised was respect as they realised that he—Ratcliffe—was unshakably convinced that Pettigrew's aim was money; that Pettigrew had invented or evolved a scheme so richly rewarding that he—Ratcliffe—had not only been unable to forestall him and do it first, he—Ratcliffe—couldn't even guess what it was after he had been given a hint) until Compson interrupted him.

'Hell,' Compson said. 'Everybody knows what's wrong with him. It's ethics. He's a damned moralist.'

'Ethics?' Peabody said. He sounded almost startled. He said quickly: 'That's bad. How can we corrupt an ethical man?'

'Who wants to corrupt him?' Compson said. 'All we want him to do is stay on that damned horse and blow whatever extra wind he's got into that damned horn.'

But Peabody was not even listening. He said, 'Ethics,' almost dreamily. He said, 'Wait.' They watched him. He said suddenly to Ratcliffe: 'I've heard it somewhere. If anybody here knows it, it'll be you. What's his name?'

'His name?' Ratcliffe said. 'Pettigrew's? Oh. His christian name.' Ratcliffe told him. 'Why?'

'Nothing,' Peabody said. 'I'm going home. Anybody else coming?' He spoke directly to nobody and said and would say no more, but that was enough: a straw perhaps, but at least a straw; enough anyway for the others to watch and say nothing either as Compson got up to and said to Ratcliffe:

'You coming?' and the three of them walked away together, beyond earshot then beyond sight too. Then Compson said, 'All right. What?'

'It may not work,' Peabody said. 'But you two will have to back me up. When I speak for the whole settlement, you and Ratcliffe will have to make it stick. Will you?'

Compson cursed. 'But at least tell us a little of what we're going to guarantee.' So Peabody told them, some of it, and the next morning entered the stall in the Holston House stable where Pettigrew was grooming his ugly hammer-headed ironmuscled horse.

'We decided not to charge that lock to old Mohataha, after all,' Peabody said.

'That so?' Pettigrew said. 'Nobody in Washington would ever catch it. Certainly not the ones that can read.'

'We're going to pay for it ourselves,' Peabody said. 'In fact, we're going to do a little more. We've got to repair that jail wall anyhow; we've got to build one wall anyway. So by building three more, we will have another room. We got to build one anyway, so that dont count. So by building an extra three-wall room, we will have another four-wall house. That will be the courthouse.' Pettigrew had been hissing gently between his teeth at each stroke of the brush, like a professional Irish groom. Now he stopped, the brush and his hand arrested in midstroke, and turned his head a little.

'Courthouse?'

'We're going to have a town,' Peabody said. 'We already got a church—that's Whitfield's cabin. And we're going to build a school too soon as we get around to it. But we're going to build the courthouse today; we've already got something to put in it to make it a courthouse: that iron box that's been in Ratcliffe's way in the store for the last ten years. Then we'll have a town. We've already even named her.'

Now Pettigrew stood up, very slowly. They looked at one another. After a moment Pettigrew said, 'So?'

'Ratcliffe says your name's Jefferson,' Peabody said.

'That's right,' Pettigrew said. 'Thomas Jefferson Pettigrew. I'm from old Ferginny.'

'Any kin?' Peabody said.

'No,' Pettigrew said. 'My ma named me for him, so I would have some of his luck.'

'Luck?' Peabody said.

Pettigrew didn't smile. 'That's right. She didn't mean luck. She never had any schooling. She didn't know the word she wanted to say.'

'Have you had it?' Peabody said. Nor did Pettigrew smile now. 'I'm sorry,' Peabody said. 'Try to forget it.' He said: 'We decided to name her Jefferson.' Now Pettigrew didn't seem to breathe even. He just stood there, small, frail, less than boysize, childless and bachelor, incorrigibly kinless and tieless, looking at Peabody. Then he breathed, and raising the brush, he turned back to the horse and for an instant Peabody thought he was going back to the grooming. But instead of making the stroke, he laid the hand and the brush against the horse's flank and stood for a moment, his face turned away and his head bent a little. Then he raised his head and turned his face back toward Peabody.

'You could call that lock 'axle grease' on that Indian account,' he said.

'Fifty dollars' worth of axle grease?' Peabody said.

'To grease the wagons for Oklahoma,' Pettigrew said.

'So we could,' Peabody said. 'Only her name's Jefferson now. We cant ever forget that any more now.' And that was the courthouse—the courthouse which it had taken them almost thirty years not only to realise they didn't have, but to discover that they hadn't even needed, missed, lacked; and which, before they had owned it six months, they discovered was nowhere near enough. Because somewhere between the dark of that first day and the dawn of the next, something happened to them. They began that same day; they restored the jail wall and cut new logs and split out shakes and raised the little floorless lean-to against it and moved the iron chest from Ratcliffe's back room; it took only the two days and cost nothing but the labor and not much of that per capita since the whole settlement was involved to a man, not to mention the settlement's two slaves—Holston's man and the one belonging to the German blacksmith—; Ratcliffe too, all he had to do was put up the bar across the inside of his back door, since his entire patronage was countable in one glance sweating and cursing among the logs and shakes of the half dismantled jail across the way opposite—including Ikkemotubbe's Chickasaw, though these were neither sweating nor cursing: the grave dark men dressed in their Sunday clothes except for the trousers, pants, which they carried rolled neatly under their arms or perhaps tied by the two legs around their necks like capes or rather hussars' dolmans where they had forded the creek, squatting or lounging along the shade, courteous, interested, and reposed (even old Mohataha herself, the matriarch, barefoot in a purple silk gown and a plumed hat, sitting in a gilt brocade empire chair in a wagon behind two mules, under a silver-handled Paris parasol held by a female slave child)—because they (the other white men, his confreres, or—during this first day—his co-victims) had not yet remarked the thing—quality—something— esoteric, eccentric, in Ratcliffe's manner, attitude,—not an obstruction nor even an impediment, not even when on the second day they discovered what it was, because he was among them, busy too, sweating and cursing too, but rather like a single chip, infinitesimal, on an otherwise unbroken flood or tide, a single body or substance, alien and unreconciled, a single thin almost unheard voice crying thinly out of the roar of a mob: 'Wait, look here, listen—'

Because they were too busy raging and sweating among the dismantled logs and felling the new ones in the adjacent woods and trimming and notching and dragging them out and mixing the tenuous clay mud to chink them together with; it was not until the second day that they learned what was troubling Ratcliffe, because now they had time, the work going no slower, no lessening of sweat but on the contrary, if anything the work going even a little faster because now there was a lightness in the speed and all that was abated was the rage and the outrage, because somewhere between the dark and the dawn of the first and the second day, something had happened to them—the men who had spent that first long hot endless July day sweating and raging about the wrecked jail, flinging indiscriminately and savagely aside the dismantled logs and the log-like laudanum-smitten inmates in order to rebuild the one, cursing old Holston and the lock and the four—three—bandits and the eleven militiamen who had arrested them, and Compson and Pettigrew and Peabody and the United States of America —the same men met at the project before sunrise on the next day which was already promising to be hot and endless too, but with the rage and the fury absent now, quiet, not grave so much as sobered, a little amazed, diffident, blinking a little perhaps, looking a little aside from one another, a little unfamiliar even to one another in the new jonquil-colored light, looking about them at the meagre huddle of crude cabins set without order and every one a little awry to every other and all dwarfed to doll-houses by the vast loom of the woods which enclosed them—the tiny clearing clawed punily not even into the flank of pathless wilderness but into the loin, the groin, the secret parts, which was the irrevocable cast die of their lives, fates, pasts and futures—not even speaking for a while yet since each one probably believed (a little shamefaced too) that the thought was solitarily his, until at last one spoke for all and then it was all right since it had taken one conjoined breath to shape that sound, the speaker speaking not loud, diffidently, tentatively, as you insert the first light tentative push of wind into the mouthpiece of a strange untried foxhorn: 'By God. Jefferson.'

'Jefferson, Mississippi,' a second added.

'Jefferson, Yoknapatawpha County, Mississippi,' a third corrected; who, which one, didn't matter this

time either since it was still one conjoined breathing,
one compound dream-state, mused and static, well capable of lasting on past sunrise too, though they probably
knew better too since Compson was still there: the gnat,
the thorn, the catalyst.

'It aint until we finish the goddamned thing,'
Compson said. 'Come on. Let's get at it.' So they finished
it that day, working rapidly now, with speed and lightness too, concentrated yet inattentive, to get it done and
that quickly, not to finish it but to get it out of the way,
behind them; not to finish it quickly in order to own,
possess it sooner, but to be able to obliterate, efface, it
the sooner, as if they had also known in that first yellow
light that it would not be near enough, would not even
be the beginning; that the little lean-to room they were
building would not even be a pattern and could not even
be called practice, working on until noon, the hour to
stop and eat, by which time Louis Grenier had arrived
from Frenchman's Bend (his plantation: his manor,
his kitchens and stables and kennels and slave quarters
and gardens and promenades and fields which a hundred years later will have vanished, his name and his
blood too, leaving nothing but the name of his plantation and his own fading corrupted legend like a thin layer
of the native ephemeral yet inevictable dust on a section
of country surrounding a little lost paintless crossroads
store) twenty miles away behind a slave coachman and
footman in his imported English carriage and what was
said to be the finest matched team outside of Natchez or

Nashville, and Compson said, 'I reckon that'll do'—all knowing what he meant: not abandonment: to complete it, of course, but so little remained now that the two slaves could finish it. The four in fact, since, although as soon as it was assumed that the two Grenier Negroes would lend the two local ones a hand, Compson demurred on the grounds that who would dare violate the rigid protocol of bondage by ordering a stable-servant, let alone a house-servant, to do manual labor, not to mention having the temerity to approach old Louis Grenier with the suggestion, Peabody nipped that at once.

'One of them can use my shadow,' he said. 'It never blenched out there with a white doctor standing in it,' and even offered to be emissary to old Grenier, except that Grenier himself forestalled them. So they ate Holston's noon ordinary, while the Chickasaws, squatting unmoving still where the creep of shade had left them in the full fierce glare of July noon about the wagon where old Mohataha still sat under her slave-borne Paris parasol, ate their lunches too which (Mohataha's and her personal retinue's came out of a woven whiteoak withe fishbasket in the wagonbed) they appeared to have carried in from what, patterning the white people, they called their plantation too, under their arms inside the rolled-up trousers. Then they moved back to the front gallery and—not the settlement any more now: the town; it had been a town for thirty-one hours now—watched the four slaves put up the final log and pin down the final shake on the roof and hang the door, and then, Ratcliffe

leading something like the court chamberlain across a
castle courtyard, cross back to the store and enter and
emerge carrying the iron chest, the grave Chickasaws
watching too the white man's slaves sweating the white
man's ponderable dense inscrutable medicine into its
new shrine. And now they had time to find out what was
bothering Ratcliffe.

'That lock,' Ratcliffe said.

'What?' somebody said.

'That Indian axle-grease,' Ratcliffe said.

'What?' they said again. But they knew, under-
stood, now. It was neither lock nor axle-grease; it was
the fifteen dollars which could have been charged to
the Indian Department on Ratcliffe's books and nobody
would have ever found it, noticed it, missed it. It was
not greed on Ratcliffe's part, and least of all was he
advocating corruption. The idea was not even new to
him; it did not need any casual man on a horse riding
in to the settlement once every two or three weeks, to reveal to him that possibility; he had thought of that the
first time he had charged the first sack of peppermint
candy to the first one of old Mohataha's forty-year-old
grandchildren and had refrained from adding two zeroes
to the ten or fifteen cents for ten years now, wondering
each time why he did refrain, amazed at his own virtue
or at least his strength of will. It was a matter of principle. It was he—they: the settlement (town now)—who
had thought of charging the lock to the United States as
a provable lock, a communal risk, a concrete ineradi-

cable object, win lose or draw, let the chips fall where
they may, on that dim day when some Federal inspector
might, just barely might, audit the Chickasaw affairs;
it was the United States itself which had voluntarily
offered to show them how to transmute the inevictable
lock into proofless and ephemeral axle grease—the
little scrawny childsized man, solitary unarmed impregnable and unalarmed, not even defying them, not
even advocate and representative of the United States,
but *the* United States, as though the United States had
said, 'Please accept a gift of fifteen dollars,' (the town
had actually paid old Alec fifteen dollars for the lock; he
would accept no more) and they had not even declined it
but simply abolished it since, as soon as Pettigrew
breathed it into sound, the United States had already
forever lost it; as though Pettigrew had put the actual
ponderable fifteen gold coins into—say, Compson's or
Peabody's—hands and they had dropped them down a
rathole or a well, doing no man any good, neither restora-
tion to the ravaged nor emolument to the ravager, leaving
in fact the whole race of man, as long as it endured, forever and irrevocably fifteen dollars deficit, fifteen dollars
in the red;

That was Ratcliffe's trouble. But they didn't even
listen. They heard him out of course, but they didn't
even listen. Or perhaps they didn't even hear him either,
sitting along the shade on Holston's gallery, looking,
seeing, already a year away; it was barely the tenth of

July; there was the long summer, the bright soft dry
fall until the November rains, but they would require
not two days this time but two years and maybe more,
with a winter of planning and preparation before hand.
They even had an instrument available and waiting,
like providence almost: a man named Sutpen who had
come into the settlement that same spring—a big gaunt
friendless passion-worn untalkative man who walked in
a fading aura of anonymity and violence like a man
just entered a warm room or at least a shelter, out of a
blizzard, bringing with him thirty-odd men slaves even
wilder and more equivocal than the native wild men,
the Chickasaws, to whom the settlement had become accustomed, who (the new Negroes) spoke no English but
instead what Compson, who had visited New Orleans,
said was the Carib-Spanish-French of the Sugar Islands,
and who (Sutpen) had bought or proved on or anyway
acquired a tract of land in the opposite direction and
was apparently bent on establishing a place on an even
more ambitious and grandiose scale than Grenier's; he
had even brought with him a tame Parisian architect—
or captive rather, since it was said in Ratcliffe's back
room that the man slept at night in a kind of pit at the
site of the chateau he was planning, tied wrist to wrist
with one of his captor's Carib slaves; indeed, the settlement had only to see him once to know that he was no
dociler than his captor, any more than the weasel or
rattlesnake is no less untame than the wolf or bear before which it gives way until completely and hopelessly

cornered:—a man no larger than Pettigrew, with humorous sardonic undefeated eyes which had seen everything
and believed none of it, in the broad expensive hat and
brocaded waistcoat and ruffled wrists of a half-artist half-
boulevardier; and they—Compson perhaps, Peabody
certainly—could imagine him in his mudstained brier-
slashed brocade and lace standing in a trackless wilderness dreaming colonnades and porticoes and fountains
and promenades in the style of David, with just behind
each elbow an identical giant half-naked Negro not even
watching him, only breathing, moving each time he took
a step or shifted like his shadow repeated in two and
blown to gigantic size;

So they even had an architect. He listened to them for
perhaps a minute in Ratcliffe's back room. Then he
made an indescribable gesture and said, 'Bah. You do
not need advice. You are too poor. You have only your
hands, and clay to make good brick. You dont have any
money. You dont even have anything to copy: how can
you go wrong?' But he taught them how to mold the
brick; he designed and built the kiln to bake the brick
in, plenty of them since they had probably known from
that first yellow morning too that one edifice was not
going to be enough. But although both were conceived
in the same instant and planned simultaneously during
the same winter and built in continuation during the
next three years, the courthouse of course came first, and
in March, with stakes and hanks of fishline, the architect laid out in a grove of oaks opposite the tavern and

the store, the square and simple foundations, the irrevocable design not only of the courthouse but of the town too, telling them as much: 'In fifty years you will be trying to change it in the name of what you will call progress. But you will fail; but you will never be able to get away from it.' But they had already seen that, standing thigh-deep in wilderness also but with more than a vision to look at since they had at least the fish-line and the stakes, perhaps less than fifty years, perhaps—who knew?—less than twenty-five even: a Square, the courthouse in its grove the center; quadrangular around it, the stores, two-storey, the offices of the lawyers and doctors and dentists, the lodge-rooms and auditoriums, above them; school and church and tavern and bank and jail each in its ordered place; the four broad diverging avenues straight as plumb-lines in the four directions, becoming the network of roads and by-roads until the whole county would be covered with it: the hands, the prehensile fingers clawing dragging lightward out of the disappearing wilderness year by year as up from the bottom of the receding sea, the broad rich fecund burgeoning fields, pushing thrusting each year further and further back the wilderness and its denizens —the wild bear and deer and turkey, and the wild men (or not so wild any more, familiar now, harmless now, just obsolete: anachronism out of an old dead time and a dead age; regrettable of course, even actually regretted by the old men, fiercely as old Doctor Habersham did, and with less fire but still as irreconcilable and stubborn as old Alec Holston and a few others were still doing, until in a few more years the last of them would have passed and vanished in their turn too, obsolescent too: because this was a white man's land; that was its fate, or not even fate but destiny, its high destiny in the roster of the earth)—the veins, arteries, life- and pulse-stream along which would flow the aggrandisement of harvest: the gold: the cotton and the grain;

But above all, the courthouse: the center, the focus, the hub; sitting looming in the center of the county's circumference like a single cloud in its ring of horizon, laying its vast shadow to the uttermost rim of horizon; musing, brooding, symbolic and ponderable, tall as cloud, solid as rock, dominating all: protector of the weak, judiciate and curb of the passions and lusts, repository and guardian of the aspirations and the hopes; rising course by brick course during that first summer, simply square, simplest Georgian colonial (this, by the Paris architect who was creating at Sutpen's Hundred something like a wing of Versailles glimpsed in a Lilliput's gothic nightmare—in revenge, Gavin Stevens would say a hundred years later, when Sutpen's own legend in the county would include the anecdote of the time the architect broke somehow out of his dungeon and tried to flee and Sutpen and his Negro head man and hunter ran him down with dogs in the swamp and brought him back) since, as the architect had told them, they had no money to buy bad taste with nor even anything from which to copy what bad taste might still have been within their compass; this one too still costing nothing but the labor and—the second year now—most of that was slave since there were still more slave owners in the settlement which had been a town and named for going on two years now, already a town and already named when the first ones waked up on that yellow morning two years back:—men other than Holston and the blacksmith (Compson was one now) who owned one or two or three Negroes, besides Grenier and Sutpen who had set up camps beside the creek in Compson's pasture for the two gangs of their Negroes to live in until the two buildings —the courthouse and the jail—should be completed. But not altogether slave, the boundmen, the unfree, because there were still the white men too, the same ones who on that hot July morning two and now three years ago had gathered in a kind of outraged unbelief to fling, hurl up in raging sweating impotent fury the little three-walled lean-to—the same men (with affairs of their own they might have been attending to or work of their own or for which they were being hired, paid, that they should have been doing) standing or lounging about the scaffolding and the stacks of brick and puddles of clay mortar for an hour or two hours or half a day, then putting aside one of the Negroes and taking his place with trowel or saw or adze, unbidden or unreproved either since there was none present with the right to order or deny; a stranger might have said probably for that reason, simply because now they didn't have to, except that it was more than that, working peacefully

now that there was no outrage and fury, and twice as
fast because there was no urgency since this was no more
to be hurried by man or men than the burgeoning of a
crop, working (this paradox too to anyone except men
like Grenier and Compson and Peabody who had grown
from infancy among slaves, breathed the same air and
even suckled the same breast with the sons of Ham: black
and white, free and unfree, shoulder to shoulder in the
same tireless lift and rhythm as if they had the same
aim and hope, which they did have as far as the Negro
was capable, as even Ratcliffe, son of a long pure line of
Anglo-Saxon mountain people and—destined—father of
an equally long and pure line of white trash tenant farmers who never owned a slave and never would since each
had and would imbibe with his mother's milk a personal
violent antipathy not at all to slavery but to black skins,
could have explained: the slave's simple child's mind
had fired at once with the thought that he was helping to
build not only the biggest edifice in the country, but
probably the biggest he had ever seen; this was all but
this was enough) as one because it was theirs, bigger
than any because it was the sum of all and, being the
sum of all, it must raise all of their hopes and aspirations level with its own aspirant and soaring cupola, so
that, sweating and tireless and unflagging, they would
look about at one another a little shyly, a little amazed,
with something like humility too, as if they were realising, or were for a moment at least capable of believing,
that men, all men, including themselves, were a little
better, purer maybe even, than they had thought, ex-

pected, or even needed to be. Though they were still having a little trouble with Ratcliffe: the money, the Holston lock-Chickasaw axle grease fifteen dollars; not trouble really because it had never been an obstruction even three years ago when it was new, and now after three years even the light impedeless chip was worn by familiarity and custom to less than a toothpick: merely present, merely visible, or that is, audible: and no trouble *with* Ratcliffe because he made one too contraposed the toothpick; more: he was its chief victim, sufferer, since where with the others was mostly inattention, a little humor, now and then a little fading annoyance and impatience, with him was shame, bafflement, a little of anguish and despair like a man struggling with a congenital vice, hopeless, indomitable, already defeated. It was not even the money any more now, the fifteen dollars. It was the fact that they had refused it and, refusing it, had maybe committed a fatal and irremediable error. He would try to explain it: 'It's like Old Moster and the rest of them up there that run the luck, would look down at us and say, Well well, looks like them durn peckerwoods down there dont want them fifteen dollars we was going to give them free-gratis-for-nothing. So maybe they dont want nothing from us. So maybe we better do like they seem to want, and let them sweat and swivet and scrabble through the best they can by themselves.'

Which they—the town—did, though even then the courthouse was not finished for another six years. Not but that they thought it was: complete: simple and square, floored and roofed and windowed, with a central hallway and the four offices—sheriff and tax assessor and circuit- and chancery-clerk (which—the chancery-clerk's office—would contain the ballot boxes and booths for voting)—below, and the courtroom and jury-room and the judge's chambers above—even to the pigeons and English sparrows, migrants too but not pioneers, inevictably urban in fact, come all the way from the Atlantic coast as soon as the town became a town with a name, taking possession of the gutters and eave-boxes almost before the final hammer was withdrawn, uxorious and interminable the one, garrulous and myriad the other. Then in the sixth year old Alec Holston died and bequeathed back to the town the fifteen dollars it had paid him for the lock; two years before, Louis Grenier had died and his heirs still held in trust on demand the fifteen hundred dollars his will had devised it, and now there was another newcomer in the county, a man named John Sartoris, with slaves and gear and money too like Grenier and Sutpen, but who was an even better stalemate to Sutpen than Grenier had been because it was apparent at once that he, Sartoris, was the sort of man who could even cope with Sutpen in the sense that a man with a sabre or even a small sword and heart enough for it could cope with one with an axe; and that summer (Sutpen's Paris architect had long since gone back to whatever place he came from and to which he had made his one abortive midnight try to return, but his trickle, flow

of bricks had never even faltered: his molds and kilns
had finished the jail and were now raising the walls of
two churches and by the half-century would have completed what would be known through all north Mississippi and east Tennessee as *the* Academy, *the* Female
Institute) there was a committee: Compson and Sartoris
and Peabody (and *in absentia* Sutpen: nor would the
town ever know exactly how much of the additional cost
Sutpen and Sartoris made up): and the next year the
eight disjointed marble columns were landed from an
Italian ship at New Orleans, into a steamboat up the
Mississippi to Vicksburg, and into a smaller steamboat
up the Yazoo and Sunflower and Tallahatchie, to Ikkemotubbe's old landing which Sutpen now owned, and thence
the twelve miles by oxen into Jefferson: the two identical
four-column porticoes, one on the north and one on the
south, each with its balcony of wroughtiron New Orleans
grillwork, on one of which—the south one—in 1861
Sartoris would stand in the first Confederate uniform the
town had ever seen, while in the Square below the Richmond mustering officer enrolled and swore in the regiment which Sartoris as its colonel would take to Virginia
as a part of Bee, to be Jackson's extreme left in front of
the Henry house at First Manassas, and from both of
which each May and November for a hundred years,
bailiffs in their orderly appointive almost hereditary succession would cry without inflection or punctuation either
'oyes oyes honorable circuit court of Yoknapatawpha
County come all and ye shall be heard' and beneath

which for that same length of time too except for the seven years between '63 and '70 which didn't really count a century afterward except to a few irreconcilable old ladies, the white male citizens of the county would pass to vote for county and state offices, because when in '63 a United States military force burned the Square and the business district, the courthouse survived. It didn't escape: it simply survived: harder than axes, tougher than fire, more fixed than dynamite; encircled by the tumbled and blackened ruins of lesser walls, it still stood, even the topless smoke-stained columns, gutted of course and roofless, but immune, not one hair even out of the Paris architect's almost forgotten plumb, so that all they had to do (it took nine years to build; they needed twenty-five to restore it) was put in new floors for the two storeys and a new roof, and this time with a cupola with a four-faced clock and a bell to strike the hours and ring alarms; by this time the Square, the banks and the stores and the lawyers' and doctors' and dentists' offices, had been restored, and the English sparrows were back too which had never really deserted—the garrulous noisy independent swarms which, as though concomitant with, inextricable from regularised and roted human quarreling, had appeared in possession of cornices and gutter-boxes almost before the last nail was driven— and now the pigeons also, interminably murmurous, nest- ing in, already usurping, the belfry even though they couldn't seem to get used to the bell, bursting out of the cupola at each stroke of the hour in frantic clouds, to sink and burst and whirl again at each succeeding stroke, until the last one: then vanishing back through the slatted louvers until nothing remained but the frantic and murmurous cooing like the fading echoes of the bell itself, the source of the alarm never recognised and even the alarm itself unremembered, as the actual stroke of the bell is no longer remembered by the vibration-fading air. Because they—the sparrows and the pigeons—endured, durable, a hundred years, the oldest things there except the courthouse centennial and serene above the town most of whose people now no longer even knew who Doctor Habersham and old Alec Holston and Louis Grenier were, had been; centennial and serene above the change: the electricity and gasoline, the neon and the crowded cacophonous air; even Negroes passing in beneath the balconies and into the chancery clerk's office to cast ballots too, voting for the same white-skinned rascals and demagogues and white supremacy champions that the white ones did—durable: every few years the county fathers, dreaming of bakshish, would instigate a movement to tear it down and erect a new modern one, but someone would at the last moment defeat them; they will try it again of course and be defeated perhaps once again or even maybe twice again, but no more than that. Because its fate is to stand in the hinterland of America: its doom is its longevity; like a man, its simple age is its own reproach, and after the hundred years, will become unbearable. But not for a little while yet; for a little while yet the sparrows and the pigeons: garrulous myriad and independent the one, the other uxorious and interminable, at once frantic and tranquil—until the clock strikes again which even after a hundred years, they still seem unable to get used to, bursting in one swirling explosion out of the belfry as though, the hour, instead of merely adding one puny infinitesimal more to the long weary increment since Genesis, had shattered the virgin pristine air with the first loud dingdong of time and doom.

Courtroom. 5:30 P.M. November thirteenth.

The curtain is down. As the lights begin to go up:

MAN'S VOICE
(behind the curtain)
Let the prisoner stand.

The curtain rises, symbolising the rising of the prisoner
in the dock, and revealing a section of the courtroom. It
does not occupy the whole stage, but only the upper left
half, leaving the other half and the bottom of the stage
in darkness, so that the visible scene is not only spot-
lighted but elevated slightly too, a further symbolism
which will be clearer when Act II opens—the symbolism
of the elevated tribunal of justice of which this, a county
court, is only the intermediate, not the highest, stage.

This is a section of the court—the bar, the judge, officers, the opposing lawyers, the jury. The defense lawyer
is Gavin Stevens, about fifty. He looks more like a poet
than a lawyer and actually is: a bachelor, descendant of
one of the pioneer Yoknapatawpha County families,
Harvard and Heidelberg educated, and returned to his
native soil to be a sort of bucolic Cincinnatus, champion
not so much of truth as of justice, or of justice as he sees
it, constantly involving himself, often for no pay, in

affairs of equity and passion and even crime too among his people, white and Negro both, sometimes directly contrary to his office of County Attorney which he has held for years, as is the present business.

The prisoner is standing. She is the only one standing in the room—a Negress, quite black, about thirty—that is, she could be almost anything between twenty and forty —with a calm impenetrable almost bemused face, the tallest, highest there with all eyes on her but she herself not looking at any of them, but looking out and up as though at some distant corner of the room, as though she were alone in it. She is—or until recently, two months ago to be exact—a domestic servant, nurse to two white children, the second of whom, an infant, she smothered in its cradle two months ago, for which act she is now on trial for her life. But she has probably done many things else—chopped cotton, cooked for working gangs—any sort of manual labor within her capacities, or rather, limitations in time and availability, since her principal reputation in the little Mississippi town where she was born is that of a tramp—a drunkard, a casual prostitute, being beaten by some man or cutting or being cut by his wife or his other sweetheart. She has probably been married, at least once. Her name—or so she calls it and would probably spell it if she could spell—is Nancy Mannigoe.

There is a dead silence in the room while everybody watches her.

JUDGE

Have you anything to say before the sentence of
the court is pronounced upon you?

Nancy neither answers nor moves; she doesn't even seem
to be listening.

That you, Nancy Mannigoe, did on the ninth day
of September, wilfully and with malice afore-
thought kill and murder the infant child of Mr
and Mrs Gowan Stevens in the town of Jefferson
and the County of Yoknapatawpha . . .

It is the sentence of this court that you be taken
from hence back to the county jail of Yoknapatawpha County and there on the thirteenth day of
March be hanged by the neck until you are dead.
And may God have mercy on your soul.

NANCY

(quite loud in the silence, to
no one, quite calm, not
moving)

Yes, Lord.

There is a gasp, a sound, from the invisible spectators in
the room, of shock at this unheard-of violation of pro-
cedure: the beginning of something which might be con-
sternation and even uproar, in the midst of, or rather
above which, Nancy herself does not move. The judge
bangs his gavel, the bailiff springs up, the curtain starts
hurriedly and jerkily down as if the judge, the officers,

the court itself were jerking frantically at it to hide this disgraceful business; from somewhere among the unseen spectators there comes the sound of a woman's voice—a moan, wail, sob perhaps.

BAILIFF
(loudly)
Order! Order in the court! Order!

The curtain descends rapidly, hiding the scene, the lights fade rapidly into darkness: a moment of darkness: then the curtain rises smoothly and normally on:

Stevens living-room. 6:00 P.M. November thirteenth.

Living-room, a center table with a lamp, chairs, a sofa
left rear, floor-lamp, wall-bracket lamps, a door left
enters from the hall, double doors rear stand open on a
dining-room, a fireplace right with gas logs. The atmos-
phere of the room is smart, modern, up-to-date, yet the
room itself has the air of another time—the high ceiling,
the cornices, some of the furniture; it has the air of being
in an old house, an ante-bellum house descended at last to
a spinster survivor who has modernised it (vide the gas
fire and the two overstuffed chairs) into apartments
rented to young couples or families who can afford to
pay that much rent in order to live on the right street
among other young couples who belong to the right
church and the country club.

Sound of feet, then the lights come on as if someone
about to enter had pressed a wall switch, then the door
left opens and Temple enters, followed by Gowan, her
husband, and the lawyer, Gavin Stevens. She is in the
middle twenties, very smart, soignée, in an open fur
coat, wearing a hat and gloves and carrying a handbag.
Her air is brittle and tense, yet controlled. Her face
shows nothing as she crosses to the center table and stops.
Gowan is three or four years older. He is almost a type;
there were many of him in America, the South, between
the two great wars: only children of financially secure

parents living in city apartment hotels, alumni of the best colleges, South or East, where they belonged to the right clubs; married now and raising families yet still alumni of their schools, performing acceptably jobs they themselves did not ask for, usually concerned with money: cotton futures, or stocks, or bonds. But this face is a little different, a little more than that. Something has happened to it—tragedy—something, against which it had had no warning, and to cope with which (as it discovered) no equipment, yet which it has accepted and is trying, really and sincerely and selflessly (perhaps for the first time in its life) to do its best with according to its code. He and Stevens wear their overcoats, carrying their hats. Stevens stops just inside the room. Gowan drops his hat onto the sofa in passing and goes on to where Temple stands at the table, stripping off one of her gloves.

TEMPLE

(takes cigarette from box on the table: mimics the prisoner; her voice, harsh, reveals for the first time repressed, controlled, hysteria)

Yes, God. Guilty, God. Thank you, God. If that's your attitude toward being hung, what else can you expect from a judge and jury except to accommodate you?

GOWAN

Stop it, Boots. Hush now. Soon as I light the fire,
I'll buy a drink.

(to Stevens)

Or maybe Gavin will do the fire while I do the
butler.

TEMPLE

(takes up lighter)

I'll do the fire. You get the drinks. Then Uncle
Gavin wont have to stay. After all, all he wants
to do is say good-bye and send me a postcard. He
can almost do that in two words, if he tries hard.
Then he can go home.

She crosses to the hearth and kneels and turns the gas
valve, the lighter ready in her other hand.

GOWAN

(anxiously)

Now, Boots.

TEMPLE

(snaps lighter, holds flame to
the jet)

Will you for God's sake please get me a drink?

GOWAN

Sure, honey.

(he turns: to Stevens)

Drop your coat anywhere.

He exits into the dining-room. Stevens does not move, watching Temple as the log takes fire.

> TEMPLE
>> (still kneeling, her back to Stevens)

If you're going to stay, why don't you sit down? Or vice versa. Backward. Only, it's the first one that's backward: if you're not sitting down, why don't you go? Let me be bereaved and vindicated, but at least let me do it in privacy, since God knows if any one of the excretions should take place in privacy, triumph should be the one—

Stevens watches her. Then he crosses to her, taking the handkerchief from his breast pocket, stops behind her and extends the handkerchief down where she can see it. She looks at it, then up at him. Her face is quite calm.

> TEMPLE

What's that for?

> STEVENS

It's all right. It's dry too.
>> (still extending the handker-
>> chief)

For tomorrow, then.

> TEMPLE
>> (rises quickly)

Oh, for cinders. On the train. We're going by air; hadn't Gowan told you? We leave from the

Memphis airport at midnight; we're driving up
after supper. Then California tomorrow morning; maybe we'll even go on to Hawaii in the
spring. No; wrong season: Canada, maybe. Lake
Louise in May and June—

> (she stops, listens a moment
> toward the dining-room
> doors)

So why the handkerchief? Not a threat, because
you dont have anything to threaten me with, do
you? And if you dont have anything to threaten
me with, I must not have anything you want, so
it cant be a bribe either, can it?

> (they both hear the sound
> from beyond the dining-
> room doors which indicates
> that Gowan is approaching.
> Temple lowers her voice
> again, rapidly)

Put it this way then. I dont know what you want,
because I dont care. Because whatever it is, you
wont get it from me.

> (the sound is near now—
> footsteps, clink of glass)

Now he'll offer you a drink, and then he'll ask
you too what you want, why you followed us
home. I've already answered you. No. If what
you came for is to see me weep, I doubt if you'll

even get that. But you certainly wont get anything else. Not from me. Do you understand that?

STEVENS

I hear you.

TEMPLE

Meaning, you dont believe it. All right, *touché*
then.

(quicker, tenser)

I refused to answer your question; now I'll ask
you one: How much do you—

(as Gowan enters, she
changes what she was saying
so smoothly in mid-sentence
that anyone entering would
not even realise that the
pitch of her voice had
altered)

—are her lawyer, she must have talked to you;
even a dope-fiend that murders a little baby must
have what she calls some excuse for it, even a
nigger dope-fiend and a white baby—or maybe
even more, a nigger dope-fiend and a white
baby—

GOWAN

I said, stop it, Boots.

He carries a tray containing a pitcher of water, a bowl
of ice, three empty tumblers and three whiskey glasses

already filled. The bottle itself protrudes from his top-coat pocket. He approaches Temple and offers the tray.

> That's right. I'm going to have one myself. For a change. After eight years. Why not?

TEMPLE

Why not?

> (looks at the tray)

Not highballs?

GOWAN

Not this one.

She takes one of the filled glasses. He offers the tray to Stevens, who takes the second one. Then he sets the tray on the table and takes up the third glass.

> Nary a drink in eight years; count 'em. So maybe this will be a good time to start again. At least, it wont be too soon.
>
> (to Stevens)
>
> Drink up. A little water behind it?

As though not aware that he had done so, he sets his untasted glass back on the tray, splashes water from the pitcher into a tumbler and hands the tumbler to Stevens as Stevens empties his glass and lowers it, taking the tumbler. Temple has not touched hers either.

Now maybe Defense Attorney Stevens will tell
us what he wants here.

STEVENS

Your wife has already told you. To say good-bye.

GOWAN

Then say it. One more for the road, and where's
your hat, huh?

He takes the tumbler from Stevens and turns back to the
table.

TEMPLE

> (sets her untasted glass back
> on the tray)

And put ice in it this time, and maybe even a
little water. But first, take Uncle Gavin's coat.

GOWAN

> (takes bottle from his pocket
> and makes a highball for
> Stevens in the tumbler)

That wont be necessary. If he could raise his arm
in a white courtroom to defend a murdering
nigger, he can certainly bend it in nothing but a
wool overcoat—at least to take a drink with the
victim's mother.

> (quickly: to Temple)

Sorry. Maybe you were right all the time, and I
was wrong. Maybe we've both got to keep on

saying things like that until we can get rid of them, some of them, a little of them—

TEMPLE

All right, why not? Here goes then.

> (she is watching, not Gowan
> but Stevens, who watches
> her in return, grave and
> soberly)

Dont forget the father too, dear.

GOWAN

> (mixing the drink)

Why should I, dear? How could I, dear? Except that the child's father is unfortunately just a man. In the eyes of the law, men are not supposed to suffer: they are merely appellants or appellees. The law is tender only of women and children —particularly of women, particularly particular of nigger dope-fiend whores who murder white children.

> (hands the highball to Stev-
> ens, who takes it)

So why should we expect Defense Attorney Stevens to be tender of a man or a woman who just happen to be the parents of the child that got murdered?

TEMPLE
(harshly)
Will you for God's sake please get through?
Then will you for God's sake please hush?

GOWAN
(quickly: turns)
Sorry.
(he turns toward her, sees
her hand empty, then sees
her full glass beside his own
on the tray)
No drink?

TEMPLE
I dont want it. I want some milk.

GOWAN
Right. Hot, of course.

TEMPLE
Please.

GOWAN
(turning)
Right. I thought of that too. I put a pan on to
heat while I was getting the drinks.
(crossing toward dining-
room exit)
Dont let Uncle Gavin get away until I get back.

Lock the door, if you have to. Or maybe just telephone that nigger freedom agent—what's his name?—

He exits. They dont move until the slap of the pantry door sounds.

                    TEMPLE
                         (rapid and hard)
How much do you know?
                         (rapidly)
Dont lie to me; dont you see there's not time?

                    STEVENS
Not time for what? Before your plane leaves tonight? She has a little time yet—four months, until March, the thirteenth of March—

                    TEMPLE
You know what I mean—her lawyer—seeing her every day—just a nigger, and you a white man —even if you needed anything to frighten her with—you could just buy it from her with a dose of cocaine or a pint of . . .
                              (she stops, stares at him, in
                              a sort of amazement, de-
                              spair; her voice is almost
                              quiet)
Oh, God, oh, God, she hasn't told you anything. It's me; I'm the one that's— Dont you see? It's

that I cannot believe—will not believe—impossible—

STEVENS

Impossible to believe that all human beings really dont—as you would put it—stink? Even —as you put it—dope-fiend nigger whores? No, she told me nothing more.

TEMPLE
(prompts)
Even if there was anything more.

STEVENS

Even if there was.

TEMPLE

Then what is it you think you know? Never mind where you got it; just tell me what you think it is.

STEVENS

There was a man there that night.

TEMPLE
(quick, glib, almost before he has finished)

Gowan.

STEVENS

That night? When Gowan had left with Bucky at six that morning to drive to New Orleans in a car?

TEMPLE

(quick, harsh)

So I was right. Did you frighten her, or just buy it?

(interrupts herself)

I'm trying. I'm really trying. Maybe it wouldn't be so hard if I could just understand why they dont stink—what reason they would have for not stinking. . . .

(she stops; it is as if she had heard a sound presaging Gowan's return, or perhaps simply knew by instinct or from knowledge of her own house that he had had time to heat a cup of milk. Then continues, rapid and quiet)

There was no man there. You see? I told you, warned you, that you would get nothing from me. Oh, I know; you could have put me on the stand at any time, under oath; of course, your jury wouldn't have liked it—that wanton crucifixion of a bereaved mamma, but what's that in the balance with justice? I dont know why you didn't. Or maybe you still intend to—provided you can catch us before we cross the Tennessee line tonight.

(quick, tense, hard)

All right. I'm sorry. I know better. So maybe it's

just my own stinking after all that I find impossible to doubt.

> (the pantry door slaps
> again; they both hear it)

Because I'm not even going to take Gowan with me when I say good-bye and go up stairs.—And who knows—

She stops. Gowan enters, carrying a small tray bearing a glass of milk, a salt-shaker and a napkin, and comes to the table.

GOWAN

What are you talking about now?

TEMPLE

Nothing. I was telling Uncle Gavin that he had something of Virginia or some sort of gentleman in him too that he must have inherited from you through your grandfather, and that I'm going up to give Bucky his bath and supper.

> (she touches the glass for
> heat, then takes it up, to
> Gowan)

Thank you, dear.

GOWAN

Right, dear.

> (to Stevens)

You see? Not just a napkin: the right napkin. That's how I'm trained.

> (he stops suddenly, noticing Temple, who has done nothing apparently: just standing there holding the milk. But he seems to know what is going on: to her)

What's this for?

TEMPLE

I dont know.

He moves; they kiss, not long but not a peck either; definitely a kiss between a man and a woman. Then, carrying the milk, Temple crosses toward the hall door.

> (to Stevens)

Good-bye then until next June. Bucky will send you and Maggie a postcard.

> (she goes on to the door, pauses and looks back at Stevens)

I may even be wrong about Temple Drake's odor too; if you should happen to hear something you haven't heard yet and it's true, I may even ratify it. Maybe you can even believe that—if you can believe you are going to hear anything that you haven't heard yet.

STEVENS

Do you?

TEMPLE
> (after a moment)

Not from me, Uncle Gavin. If someone wants to go to heaven, who am I to stop them? Good night. Good-bye.

She exits, closes the door. Stevens, very grave, turns back and sets his highball down on the tray.

GOWAN

Drink up. After all, I've got to eat supper and do some packing too. How about it?

STEVENS

About what? The packing, or the drink? What about you? I thought you were going to have one.

GOWAN

Oh, sure, sure.
> (takes up the small filled
> glass)

Maybe you had better go on and leave us to our revenge.

STEVENS

I wish it could comfort you.

GOWAN

I wish to God it could. I wish to God that what I wanted was only revenge. An eye for an eye—

were ever words emptier? Only, you have got to have lost the eye to know it.

STEVENS

Yet she still has to die.

GOWAN

Why not? Even if she would be any loss—a nigger whore, a drunkard, a dope-fiend—

STEVENS

—a vagabond, a tramp, hopeless until one day Mr and Mrs Gowan Stevens out of simple pity and humanity picked her up out of the gutter to give her one more chance—

> (Gowan stands motionless, his hand tightening slowly about the glass. Stevens watches him)

And then in return for it—

GOWAN

Look, Uncle Gavin. Why dont you go for God's sake home? Or to hell, or anywhere out of here?

STEVENS

I am, in a minute. Is that why you think—why you would still say she has to die?

GOWAN

I dont. I had nothing to do with it. I wasn't even the plaintiff. I didn't even instigate—that's the word, isn't it?—the suit. My only connection with it was, I happened by chance to be the father of the child she— Who in hell ever called that a drink?

He dashes the whiskey, glass and all, into the ice bowl, quickly catches up one of the empty tumblers in one hand and, at the same time, tilts the whiskey bottle over it, pouring. At first he makes no sound, but at once it is obvious that he is laughing: laughter which begins normally enough, but almost immediately it is out of hand, just on hysteria, while he still pours whiskey into the glass, which in a moment now will overflow, except that Stevens reaches his hand and grasps the bottle and stops it.

STEVENS

Stop it. Stop it, now. Here.

He takes the bottle from Gowan, sets it down, takes the tumbler and tilts part of its contents into the other empty one, leaving at least a reasonable, a believable, drink, and hands it to Gowan. Gowan takes it, stopping the crazy laughter, gets hold of himself again.

GOWAN

(holding the glass untasted)
Eight years. Eight years on the wagon—and this

is what I got for it: my child murdered by a dope-fiend nigger whore that wouldn't even run so that a cop or somebody could have shot her down like the mad-dog—You see? Eight years without the drink, and so I got whatever it was I was buying by not drinking, and now I've got whatever it was I was paying for and it's paid for and so I can drink again. And now I dont want the drink. You see? Like whatever it was I was buying I not only didn't want, but what I was paying for it wasn't worth anything, wasn't even any loss. So I have a laugh coming. That's triumph. Because I got a bargain even in what I didn't want. I got a cut rate. I had two children. I had to pay only one of them to find out it wasn't really costing me anything— Half price: a child, and a dope-fiend nigger whore on a public gallows: that's all I had to pay for immunity.

STEVENS
There's no such thing.

GOWAN
From the past. From my folly. My drunkenness. My cowardice, if you like—

STEVENS
There's no such thing as past either.

GOWAN
That is a laugh, that one. Only, not so loud, huh? to disturb the ladies—disturb Miss Drake—Miss

Temple Drake.—Sure, why not cowardice. Only, for euphony, call it simple over-training. You know? Gowan Stevens, trained at Virginia to drink like a gentleman, gets drunk as ten gentlemen, takes a country college girl, a maiden: who knows? maybe even a virgin, cross country by car to another country college ball game, gets drunker than twenty gentlemen, gets lost, gets still drunker than forty gentlemen, wrecks the car, passes eighty gentlemen now, passes completely out while the maiden the virgin is being kidnapped into a Memphis whorehouse—

> (he mumbles an indistinguishable word)

STEVENS

What?

GOWAN

Sure; cowardice. Call it cowardice; what's a little euphony between old married people?

STEVENS

Not the marrying her afterward, at least. What—

GOWAN

Sure. Marrying her was purest Old Virginia. That was indeed the hundred and sixty gentlemen.

STEVENS

The intent was, by any other standards too. The
prisoner in the whorehouse; I didn't quite hear—

GOWAN

(quickly: reaching for it)
Where's your glass? Dump that slop—here—

STEVENS

(holds glass)
This will do. What was that you said about held
prisoner in the whorehouse?

GOWAN

(harshly)
That's all. You heard it.

STEVENS

You said 'and loved it.'
(they stare at each other)
Is that what you can never forgive her for?—
not for having been the instrument creating that
moment in your life which you can never recall
nor forget nor explain nor condone nor even stop
thinking about, but because she herself didn't
even suffer, but on the contrary, even liked it—
that month or whatever it was like the episode in
the old movie of the white girl held prisoner in
the cave by the Bedouin prince?—That you had

to lose not only your bachelor freedom, but your man's self-respect in the chastity of his wife and your child too, to pay for something your wife hadn't even lost, didn't even regret, didn't even miss? Is that why this poor lost doomed crazy Negro woman must die?

GOWAN
(tensely)

Get out of here. Go on.

STEVENS

In a minute.—Or else, blow your own brains out: stop having to remember, stop having to be forever unable to forget: nothing; to plunge into nothing and sink and drown forever and forever, never again to have to remember, never again to wake in the night writhing and sweating because you cannot, can never not, stop remembering? What else happened during that month, that time while that madman held her prisoner there in that Memphis house, that nobody but you and she know about, maybe not even you know about?

Still staring at Stevens, slowly and deliberately Gowan sets the glass of whiskey back on the tray and takes up the bottle and swings it bottom up back over his head. The stopper is out, and at once the whiskey begins to pour out of it, down his arm and sleeve and onto the floor. He does not seem to be aware of it even. His voice is tense, barely articulate.

GOWAN

So help me, Christ . . . So help me, Christ.

A moment, then Stevens moves, without haste, sets his own glass back on the tray and turns, taking his hat as he passes the sofa, and goes on to the door and exits. Gowan stands a moment longer with the poised bottle, now empty. Then he draws a long shuddering breath, seems to rouse, wake, sets the empty bottle back on the tray, notices his untasted whiskey glass, takes it up, a moment: then turns and throws the glass crashing into the fireplace, against the burning gas logs, and stands, his back to the audience, and draws another long shuddering breath and then draws both hands hard down his face, then turns, looking at his wet sleeve, takes out his handkerchief and dabs at his sleeve as he comes back to the table, puts the handkerchief back in his pocket and takes the folded napkin from the small tray beside the saltcellar and wipes his sleeve with it, sees he is doing no good, tosses the crumpled napkin back onto the whiskey tray; and now, outwardly quite calm again, as though nothing had happened, he gathers the glasses back onto the big tray, puts the small tray and the napkin onto it too and takes up the tray and walks quietly toward the dining-room door as the lights begin to go down.

The lights go completely down. The stage is dark.

The lights go up.

Stevens living-room. 10:00 P.M. March eleventh
The room is exactly as it was four months ago, except
that the only light burning is the lamp on the table, and
the sofa has been moved so that it partly faces the audience, with a small motionless blanket-wrapped object
lying on it, and one of the chairs placed between the
lamp and the sofa so that the shadow of its back falls
across the object on the sofa, making it more or less in-
distinguishable, and the dining-room doors are now
closed. The telephone sits on the small stand in the corner right as in Scene Two.

The hall door opens. Temple enters, followed by Stevens. She now wears a long housecoat; her hair is tied back
with a ribbon as though prepared for bed. This time
Stevens carries the topcoat and the hat too; his suit is
different. Apparently she has already warned Stevens
to be quiet; his air anyway shows it. She enters, stops,
lets him pass her. He pauses, looks about the room,
sees the sofa, stands looking at it.

STEVENS

This is what they call a plant.

He crosses to the sofa, Temple watching him, and stops,
looking down at the shadowed object. He quietly draws
aside the shadowing chair and reveals a little boy, about
four, wrapped in the blanket, asleep.

TEMPLE

Why not? Dont the philosophers and other gynecologists tell us that women will strike back with any weapon, even their children?

STEVENS

(watching the child)

Including the sleeping pill you told me you gave Gowan?

TEMPLE

All right.

(approaches table)

If I would just stop struggling: how much time we could save. I came all the way back from California, but I still cant seem to quit. Do you believe in coincidence?

STEVENS

(turns)

Not unless I have to.

TEMPLE

(at table, takes up a folded yellow telegraph form, opens it, reads)

Dated Jefferson, March sixth. 'You have a week yet until the thirteenth. But where will you go then?' signed Gavin.

She folds the paper back into its old creases, folds it still again. Stevens watches her.

STEVENS

Well? This is the eleventh. Is that the coincidence?

TEMPLE

No. This is.

> (she drops, tosses the folded
> paper onto the table, turns)

It was that afternoon—the sixth. We were on the beach, Bucky and I. I was reading, and he was—oh, talking mostly, you know—'Is California far from Jefferson, mamma?' and I say 'Yes, darling'—you know: still reading or trying to, and he says, 'How long will we stay in California, mamma?' and I say, 'Until we get tired of it' and he says, 'Will we stay here until they hang Nancy, mamma?' and it's already too late then; I should have seen it coming but it's too late now; I say, 'Yes, darling' and then he drops it right in my lap, right out of the mouths of—how is it?—babes and sucklings. 'Where will we go then, mamma?' And then we come back to the hotel, and there you are too. Well?

STEVENS

Well what?

TEMPLE

All right. Let's for God's sake stop.

(goes to a chair)

Now that I'm here, no matter whose fault it was, what do you want? A drink? Will you drink? At least, put your coat and hat down.

STEVENS

I dont even know yet. That's why you came back—

TEMPLE

(interrupts)

I came back? It wasn't I who—

STEVENS

(interrupts)

—who said, let's for God's sake stop.

They stare at each other: a moment.

TEMPLE

All right. Put down your coat and hat.

Stevens lays his hat and coat on a chair. Temple sits down. Stevens takes a chair opposite, so that the sleeping child on the sofa is between them in background.

TEMPLE

So Nancy must be saved. So you send for me, or you and Bucky between you, or anyway here you are and here I am. Because apparently I know something I haven't told yet, or maybe you

know something I haven't told yet. What do you
think you know?

> (quickly; he says nothing)

All right. What do you know?

STEVENS

Nothing. I dont want to know it. All I—

TEMPLE

Say that again.

STEVENS

Say what again?

TEMPLE

What is it you think you know?

STEVENS

Nothing. I—

TEMPLE

All right. Why do you think there is something I
haven't told yet?

STEVENS

You came back. All the way from California—

TEMPLE

Not enough. Try again.

STEVENS

You were there.

> (with her face averted, Temple reaches her hand to the table, fumbles until she finds the cigarette box, takes a cigarette and with the same hand fumbles until she finds the lighter, draws them back to her lap)

At the trial. Every day. All day, from the time court opened—

TEMPLE

> (still not looking at him, supremely casual, puts the cigarette into her mouth, talking around it, the cigarette bobbing)

The bereaved mother—

STEVENS

Yes, the bereaved mother—

TEMPLE

> (the cigarette bobbing: still not looking at him)

—herself watching the accomplishment of her revenge; the tigress over the body of her slain cub—

STEVENS

—who should have been too immersed in grief
to have thought of revenge—to have borne the
very sight of her child's murderer . . .

TEMPLE

(not looking at him)

Methinks she doth protest too much?

Stevens doesn't answer. She snaps the lighter on, lights
the cigarette, puts the lighter back on the table. Leaning,
Stevens pushes the ashtray along the table until she can
reach it. Now she looks at him.

TEMPLE

Thanks. Now let grandmamma teach you how to
suck an egg. It doesn't matter what I know, what
you think I know, what might have happened.
Because we wont even need it. All we need is an
affidavit. That she is crazy. Has been for years.

STEVENS

I thought of that too. Only it's too late. That
should have been done about five months ago.
The trial is over now. She has been convicted
and sentenced. In the eyes of the law, she is already dead. In the eyes of the law, Nancy Mannigoe doesn't even exist. Even if there wasn't a
better reason than that. The best reason of all.

> **TEMPLE**
> (smoking)

Yes?

> **STEVENS**

We haven't got one.

> **TEMPLE**
> (smoking)

Yes?

> (she sits back in the chair, smoking rapidly, looking at Stevens. Her voice is gentle, patient, only a little too rapid, like the smoking)

That's right. Try to listen. Really try. I am the affidavit; what else are we doing here at ten oclock at night barely a day from her execution? What else did I—as you put it—come all the way back from California for, not to mention a—as you have probably put that too—faked coincidence to save—as I would put it I suppose—my face? All we need now is to decide just how much of what to put in the affidavit. Do try; maybe you had better have a drink after all.

> **STEVENS**

Later, maybe. I'm dizzy enough right now with just perjury and contempt of court.

TEMPLE

What perjury?

STEVENS

Not venal then, worse: inept. After my client is not only convicted but sentenced, I turn up with the prosecution's chief witness offering evidence to set the whole trial aside—

TEMPLE

Tell them I forgot this. Or tell them I changed my mind. Tell them the district attorney bribed me to keep my mouth shut—

STEVENS

(peremptory yet quiet)

Temple.

She puffs rapidly at the cigarette, removes it from her mouth.

TEMPLE

Or better still; wont it be obvious? a woman whose child was smothered in its crib, wanting vengeance, capable of anything to get the vengeance; then when she has it, realising she cant go through with it, cant sacrifice a human life for it, even a nigger whore's?

STEVENS

Stop it. One at a time. At least, let's talk about the same thing.

TEMPLE

What else are we talking about except saving a condemned client whose trained lawyer has already admitted that he has failed?

STEVENS

Then you really dont want her to die. You did invent the coincidence.

TEMPLE

Didn't I just say so? At least, let's for God's sake stop that, cant we?

STEVENS

Done. So Temple Drake will have to save her.

TEMPLE

Mrs Gowan Stevens will.

STEVENS

Temple Drake.

She stares at him, smoking, deliberately now. Deliberately she removes the cigarette and, still watching him, reaches and snubs it out in the ashtray.

STEVENS

All right. Tell me again. Maybe I'll even understand this time, let alone listen. We produce—

turn up with—a sworn affidavit that this murderess was crazy when she committed the crime.

TEMPLE

You did listen, didn't you? Who knows—·

STEVENS

Based on what?

TEMPLE

—What?

STEVENS

The affidavit. Based on what?
                    (she stares at him)
On what proof?

TEMPLE

Proof?

STEVENS

Proof. What will be in the affidavit? What are
we going to affirm now that for some reason, any
reason, we—you—we didn't see fit to bring up
or anyway didn't bring up until after she—

TEMPLE

How do I know? You're the lawyer. What do you
want in it? What do such affidavits have in them,

need to have in them, to make them work, make them sure to work? Dont you have samples in your law books—reports, whatever you call them—that you can copy and have me swear to? Good ones, certain ones? At least, while we're committing whatever this is, pick out a good one, such a good one that nobody, not even an untrained lawyer, can punch holes in it. . . .

Her voice ceases. She stares at him, while he continues to look steadily back at her, saying nothing, just looking at her, until at last she draws a loud harsh breath; her voice is harsh too.

TEMPLE

What do you want then? What more do you want?

STEVENS

Temple Drake.

TEMPLE

(quick, harsh, immediate)
No. Mrs Gowan Stevens.

STEVENS

(implacable and calm)
Temple Drake. The truth.

TEMPLE

Truth? We're trying to save a condemned murderess whose lawyer has already admitted that he has failed. What has truth got to do with that?

(rapid, harsh)

We? I, *I*, the mother of the baby she murdered; not you, Gavin Stevens, the lawyer, but I, Mrs Gowan Stevens, the mother. Cant you get it through your head that I will do anything, *anything*?

STEVENS

Except one. Which is all. We're not concerned with death. That's nothing: any handful of petty facts and sworn documents can cope with that. That's all finished now; we can forget it. What we are trying to deal with now is injustice. Only truth can cope with that. Or love.

TEMPLE

(harshly)

Love. Oh, God. Love.

STEVENS

Call it pity then. Or courage. Or simple honor honesty, or a simple desire for the right to sleep at night.

TEMPLE

You prate of sleep, to me, who learned six years

ago how not even to realise any more that I didn't mind not sleeping at night?

STEVENS

Yet you invented the coincidence.

TEMPLE

Will you for Christ's sake stop? Will you . . . All right. Then if her dying is nothing, what do you want? What in God's name do you want?

STEVENS

I told you. Truth.

TEMPLE

And I told you that what you keep on harping at as truth has nothing to do with this. When you go before the— What do you call this next collection of trained lawyers? supreme court?—what you will need will be facts, papers, documents, sworn to, incontrovertible, that no other lawyer trained or untrained either can punch holes in, find any flaw in.

STEVENS

We're not going to the supreme court.
                    (she stares at him)
That's all finished. If that could have been done, would have sufficed, I would have thought of that,

attended to that, four months ago. We're going
to the Governor. Tonight.

TEMPLE

The Governor?

STEVENS

Perhaps he wont save her either. He probably
wont.

TEMPLE

They why ask him? Why?

STEVENS

I've told you. Truth.

TEMPLE

(in quiet amazement)

For no more than that. For no better reason than
that. Just to get it told, breathed aloud, into
words, sound. Just to be heard by, told to, someone, anyone, any stranger none of whose business
it is, can possibly be, simply because he is capable of hearing, comprehending it. Why blink
your own rhetoric? Why dont you go on and tell
me it's for the good of my soul—if I have one?

STEVENS

I did. I said, so you can sleep at night.

TEMPLE

And I told you I forgot six years ago even what
it was to miss the sleep.

She stares at him. He doesn't answer, looking at her.
Still watching him, she reaches her hand to the table,
toward the cigarette box, then stops, is motionless, her
hand suspended, staring at him.

TEMPLE

There is something else, then. We're even going
to get the true one this time. All right. Shoot.

He doesn't answer, makes no sign, watching her. A moment: then she turns her head and looks toward the sofa
and the sleeping child. Still looking at the child, she rises
and crosses to the sofa and stands looking down at the
child; her voice is quiet.

TEMPLE

So it was a plant, after all; I just didn't seem to
know for who.

(she looks down at the child)

I threw my remaining child at you. Now you
threw him back.

STEVENS

But I didn't wake him.

TEMPLE

Then I've got you, lawyer. What would be better

for his peace and sleep than to hang his sister's murderer?

STEVENS

No matter by what means, in what lie?

TEMPLE

Nor whose.

STEVENS

Yet you invented the coincidence.

TEMPLE

Mrs Gowan Stevens did.

STEVENS

Temple Drake did. Mrs Gowan Stevens is not even fighting in this class. This is Temple Drake's.

TEMPLE

Temple Drake is dead.

STEVENS

The past is never dead. It's not even past.

She comes back to the table, takes a cigarette from the box, puts it in her mouth and reaches for the lighter. He leans as though to hand it to her, but she has already found it, snaps it on and lights the cigarette, talking through the smoke.

TEMPLE

Listen. How much do you know?

STEVENS

Nothing.

TEMPLE

Swear.

STEVENS

Would you believe me?

TEMPLE

No. But swear anyway.

STEVENS

All right. I swear.

TEMPLE

        (crushes cigarette into tray)
Then listen. Listen carefully.
        (she stands, tense, rigid,
        facing him, staring at him)
Temple Drake is dead. Temple Drake will have
been dead six years longer than Nancy Mannigoe will ever be. If all Nancy Mannigoe has to
save her is Temple Drake, then God help Nancy
Mannigoe. Now get out of here.

She stares at him; another moment. Then he rises, still
watching her; she stares steadily and implacably back.
Then he moves.

TEMPLE

Good night.

STEVENS

Good night.

He goes back to the chair, takes up his coat and hat, then goes on to the hall door, has put his hand on the knob.

TEMPLE

Gavin.

> (he pauses, his hand on the knob, and looks back at her)

Maybe I'll have the handkerchief, after all.

> (he looks at her a moment longer, then releases the knob, takes the handkerchief from his breast pocket as he crosses back toward her, extends it. She doesn't take it)

All right. What will I have to do? What do you suggest, then?

STEVENS

Everything.

TEMPLE

Which of course I wont. I will not. You can understand that, cant you? At least you can hear it. So let's start over, shall we? How much will I have to tell?

STEVENS

Everything.

TEMPLE

Then I wont need the handkerchief, after all.
Good night. Close the front door when you go
out, please. It's getting cold again.

He turns, crosses again to the door without stopping nor
looking back, exits, closes the door behind him. She is
not watching him either now. For a moment after the
door has closed, she doesn't move. Then she makes a
gesture something like Gowan's in Scene Two, except
that she merely presses her palms for a moment hard
against her face, her face calm, expressionless, cold,
drops her hands, turns, picks up the crushed cigarette
from beside the tray and puts it into the tray and takes
up the tray and crosses to the fireplace, glancing down
at the sleeping child as she passes the sofa, empties the
tray into the fireplace and returns to the table and puts
the tray on it and this time pauses at the sofa and stoops
and tucks the blanket closer about the sleeping child and
then goes on to the telephone and lifts the receiver.

TEMPLE

(into the phone)

Two three nine, please.

> (while she stands waiting
> for the answer, there is a
> slight movement in the dark-
> ness beyond the open door
> at rear, just enough silent

(movement to show that something or someone is there or has moved there. Temple is unaware of it since her back is turned. Then she speaks into the phone)

Maggie? Temple. . . . Yes, suddenly . . . Oh, I dont know; perhaps we got bored with sunshine. . . . Of course, I may drop in tomorrow. I wanted to leave a message for Gavin . . . I know; he just left here. Something I forgot . . . If you'll ask him to call me when he comes in. . . . Yes. . . . Wasn't it. . . . Yes. . . . If you will . . . Thank you.

(she puts the receiver down and starts to turn back into the room when the telephone rings. She turns back, takes up the receiver, speaks into it)

Hello . . . Yes. Coincidence again; I had my hand on it; I had just called Maggie. . . . Oh, the filling station. I didn't think you had had time. I can be ready in thirty minutes. Your car, or ours? . . . All right. Listen. . . . Yes, I'm here. Gavin . . . How much will I have to tell?

(hurriedly)

Oh, I know: you've already told me eight or ten times. But maybe I didn't hear it right. How much will I have to tell?

(she listens a moment,
quiet, frozen-faced, then
slowly begins to lower the
receiver toward the stand;
she speaks quietly, without
inflection)

Oh, God. Oh, God.

(She puts the receiver down, crosses to the sofa, snaps
off the table lamp and takes up the child and crosses to
the door to the hall, snaps off the remaining room lights
as she goes out, so that the only light in the room now
enters from the hall. As soon as she has disappeared
from sight, Gowan enters from the door at rear, dressed
except for his coat, vest and tie. He has obviously taken
no sleeping pill. He goes to the phone and stands quietly
beside it, facing the hall door and obviously listening
until Temple is safely away. Now the hall light snaps
off, and the stage is in complete darkness.

GOWAN'S VOICE
(quietly)

Two three nine, please . . . Good evening, Aunt
Maggie. Gowan . . . All right, thank you . . .
Sure, some time tomorrow. As soon as Uncle
Gavin comes in, will you have him call me? I'll
be right here. Thank you.

(Sound of the receiver as he puts it back)

(Curtain)

ACT TWO

THE GOLDEN DOME (Beginning Was the Word)

JACKSON. Alt. 294 ft. Pop. (A.D.1950) 201,092.
Located by an expedition of three Commissioners selected appointed and dispatched for that single purpose,
on a high bluff above Pearl River at the approximate
geographical center of the State, to be not a market nor
industrial town, nor even as a place for men to live, but
to be a capital, the Capital of a Commonwealth;

In the beginning was already decreed this rounded
knob, this gilded pustule, already before and beyond the
steamy chiaroscuro, untimed unseasoned winterless
miasma not any one of water or earth or life yet all of
each, inextricable and indivisible; that one seethe one
spawn one mother-womb, one furious tumescence, father-
mother-one, one vast incubant ejaculation already fission-
ating in one boiling moil of litter from the celestial
experimental Work Bench; that one spawning crawl and
creep printing with three-toed mastodonic tracks the
steamy-green swaddling clothes of the coal and the oil,
above which the pea-brained reptilian heads curved the
heavy leather-flapped air;

Then the ice, but still this knob, this pimple-dome, this
buried half-ball hemisphere; the earth lurched, heaving
darkward the long continental flank, dragging upward
beneath the polar cap that furious equatorial womb, the

shutter-lid of cold severing off into blank and heedless void one last sound, one cry, one puny myriad indictment already fading and then no more, the blind and tongueless earth spinning on, looping the long recordless astral orbit, frozen, tideless, yet still was there this tiny gleam, this spark, this gilded crumb of man's eternal aspiration, this golden dome preordained and impregnable, this minuscule foetus-glint tougher than ice and harder than freeze; the earth lurched again, sloughing; the ice with infinitesimal speed, scouring out the valleys, scoring the hills, and vanished; the earth tilted further to recede the sea rim by necklace-rim of crustacean husks in recessional contour lines like the concentric whorls within the sawn stump telling the tree's age, bearing south by recessional south toward that mute and beckoning gleam the confluent continental swale, baring to light and air the broad blank mid-continental page for the first scratch of orderly recording—a laboratory-factory covering what would be twenty states, established and ordained for the purpose of manufacturing one: the ordered unhurried whirl of seasons, of rain and snow and freeze and thaw and sun and drouth to aereate and slack the soil, the conflux of a hundred rivers into one vast father of rivers carrying the rich dirt, the rich garnering, south and south, carving the bluffs to bear the long march of the river towns, flooding the Mississippi lowlands, spawning the rich alluvial dirt layer by vernal layer, raising inch by foot by year by century the surface of the earth which in time (not distant now, measured against that long

signatureless chronicle) would tremble to the passing of
trains like when the cat crosses the suspension bridge;

The rich deep black alluvial soil which would grow
cotton taller than the head of a man on a horse, already
one jungle one brake one impassable density of brier
and cane and vine interlocking the soar of gum and
cypress and hickory and pinoak and ash, printed now
by the tracks of unalien shapes—bear and deer and
panthers and bison and wolves and alligators and the
myriad smaller beasts, and unalien men to name them
too perhaps—the (themselves) nameless though recorded predecessors who built the mounds to escape the
spring floods and left their meagre artifacts: the obsolete
and the dispossessed, dispossessed by those who were
dispossessed in turn because they too were obsolete: the
wild Algonquian, Chickasaw and Choctaw and Natchez
and Pascagoula, peering in virgin astonishment down
from the tall bluffs at a Chippeway canoe bearing three
Frenchmen—and had barely time to whirl and look
behind him at ten and then a hundred and then a thousand Spaniards come overland from the Atlantic Ocean:
a tide, a wash, a thrice flux-and-ebb of motion so rapid
and quick across the land's slow alluvial chronicle as tc
resemble the limber flicking of the magician's one hand
before the other holding the deck of inconstant cards:
the Frenchman for a moment, then the Spaniard for perhaps two, then the Frenchman for another two and then
the Spaniard again for another and then the Frenchman

for that one last second, half-breath; because then came the Anglo-Saxon, the pioneer, the tall man, roaring with Protestant scripture and boiled whiskey, Bible and jug in one hand and (like as not) a native tomahawk in the other, brawling, turbulent not through viciousness but simply because of his over-revved glands; uxorious and polygamous: a married invincible bachelor, dragging his gravid wife and most of the rest of his mother-in-law's family behind him into the trackless infested forest, spawning that child as like as not behind the barricade of a rifle-crotched log mapless leagues from nowhere and then getting her with another one before reaching his final itch-footed destination, and at the same time scattering his ebullient seed in a hundred dusky bellies through a thousand miles of wilderness; innocent and gullible, without bowels for avarice or compassion or forethought either, changing the face of the earth: felling a tree which took two hundred years to grow, in order to extract from it a bear or a capful of wild honey;

Obsolete too: still felling the two-hundred-year-old tree when the bear and the wild honey were gone and there was nothing in it any more but a raccoon or a possum whose hide was worth at the most two dollars, turning the earth into a howling waste from which he would be the first to vanish, not even on the heels but synchronous with the slightly darker wild men whom he had dispossessed, because, like them, only the wilderness could feed and nourish him; and so disappeared, strutted his roaring eupeptic hour, and was no more, leaving his ghost, pariah and proscribed, scriptureless now and armed only with the highwayman's, the murderer's, pistol, haunting the fringes of the wilderness which he himself had helped to destroy, because the river towns marched now recessional south by south along the processional bluffs: St Louis, Paducah, Memphis, Helena, Vicksburg, Natchez, Baton Rouge, peopled by men with mouths full of law, in broadcloth and flowered waistcoats, who owned Negro slaves and Empire beds and buhl cabinets and ormolu clocks, who strolled and smoked their cigars along the bluffs beneath which in the shanty and flatboat purlieus he rioted out the last of his doomed evening, losing his worthless life again and again to the fierce knives of his drunken and worthless kind—this in the intervals of being pursued and harried in his vanishing avatars of Harpe and Hare and Mason and Murrel, either shot on sight or hoicked, dragged out of what remained of his secret wilderness haunts along the overland Natchez trace (one day someone brought a curious seed into the land and inserted it into the earth, and now vast fields of white not only covered the waste places which with his wanton and heedless axe he had made, but were effacing, thrusting back the wilderness even faster than he had been able to, so that he barely had a screen for his back when, crouched in his thicket, he glared at his dispossessor in impotent and incredulous and uncomprehending rage) into the towns to his formal

apotheosis in a courtroom and then a gallows or the
limb of a tree;

Because those days were gone, the old brave innocent
tumultuous eupeptic tomorrowless days; the last broad-
horn and keelboat (Mike Fink was a legend; soon even
the grandfathers would no longer claim to remember
him, and the river hero was now the steamboat gambler
wading ashore in his draggled finery from the towhead
where the captain had marooned him) had been sold
piecemeal for firewood in Chartres and Toulouse and
Dauphine street, and Choctaw and Chickasaw braves, in
short hair and overalls and armed with mule-whips in
place of war-clubs and already packed up to move west
to Oklahoma, watched steamboats furrowing even the
shallowest and remotest wilderness streams where tumbled gently to the motion of the paddle-wheels, the gutted
rock-weighted bones of Hare's and Mason's murderees;
a new time, a new age, millennium's beginning; one vast
single net of commerce webbed and veined the mid-
continent's fluvial embracement; New Orleans, Pittsburgh, and Fort Bridger, Wyoming, were suburbs one to
the other, inextricable in destiny; men's mouths were
full of law and order, all men's mouths were round with
the sound of money; one unanimous golden affirmation
ululated the nation's boundless immeasurable forenoon:
profit plus regimen equals security: a nation of commonwealths; that crumb, that dome, that gilded pustule, that
Idea risen now, suspended like a balloon or a portent or

a thundercloud above what used to be wilderness, drawing, holding the eyes of all: Mississippi: a state, a commonwealth; triumvirate in legislative, judiciary, executive, but without a capital, functioning as though from a
field headquarters, operating as though still en route
toward that high inevitable place in the galaxy of commonwealths, so in 1820 from its field p.c. at Columbia
the legislature selected appointed and dispatched the
three Commissioners Hinds, Lattimore and Patton, not
three politicians and less than any three political time-
servers but soldiers engineers and patriots—soldier to
cope with the reality, engineer to cope with the aspiration, patriot to hold fast to the dream—three white men
in a Choctaw pirogue moving slowly up the empty
reaches of a wilderness river as two centuries ago the
three Frenchmen had drifted in their Northern birchbark
down that vaster and emptier one;

But not drifting, these: paddling: because this was up-
stream, bearing not volitionless into the unknown mys-
tery and authority, but establishing in the wilderness a
point for men to rally to in conscience and free will,
scanning, watching the dense inscrutable banks in their
turn too, conscious of the alien incorrigible eyes too
perhaps but already rejectant of them, not that the wilderness's dark denizens, already dispossessed at Doak's
Stand, were less inveterate now, but because this canoe
bore not the meek and bloody cross of Christ and Saint
Louis, but the scales the blindfold and the sword—up

the river to Le Fleur's Bluff, the trading-post store on
the high mild promontory established by the Canadian
voyageur, whose name, called and spelled 'Leflore' now,
would be borne by the half-French half-Choctaw hereditary first chief of the Choctaw nation who, siding with
the white men at the Council of Dancing Rabbit, would
remain in Mississippi after his people departed for the
west, to become in time among the first of the great slave-
holding cotton planters and leave behind him a county
and its seat named for himself and a plantation named in
honor of a French king's mistress—stopping at last
though still paddling slowly to hold the pirogue against
the current, looking not up at the dark dispossessed faces
watching them from the top of the bluff, but looking
staring rather from one to another among themselves in
the transfixed boat, saying, 'This is the city. This is the
State';

1821, General Hinds and his co-commissioners, with
Abraham DeFrance, superintendent of public buildings
at Washington, to advise them, laid out the city according to Thomas Jefferson's plan to Territorial Governor
Claiborne seventeen years ago, and built the statehouse,
thirty by forty feet of brick and clay and native lime-
stone yet large enough to contain the dream; the first
legislature convened in it in the new year 1822;

And named the city after the other old hero, hero Hinds'
brother-in-arms on beaten British and Seminole fields

and presently to be President—the old duellist, the brawling lean fierce mangy durable old lion who set the well-being of the Nation above the White House, and the health of his new political party above either, and above them all set, not his wife's honor, but the principle that honor must be defended whether it was or not since, defended, it was, whether or not;—Jackson, that the new city created not for a city but a central point for the governance of men, might partake of the successful soldier's courage and endurance and luck, and named the area surrounding it 'Hinds County' after the lesser hero, as the hero's quarters, even empty, not only partake of his dignity but even guard and increase its stature;

And needed them, the luck at least: in 1829 the Senate passed a bill authorising the removal of the capital to Clinton, the House defeated it; in 1830 the House itself voted to move to Port Gibson on the Mississippi, but with the next breath reconsidered, reneged, the following day they voted to move to Vicksburg but nothing came of that either, no records (Sherman burned them in 1863 and notified his superior, General Grant, by note of hand with comfortable and encouraging brevity.) to show just what happened this time: a trial, a dry run perhaps or perhaps still enchannelled by a week's or a month's rut of habit or perhaps innocent in juvenility, absent or anyway missing the unanimous voice or presence of the three patriot-dreamers who forced the current and bore the dream, like a child with dynamite: innocent of its own power for alteration: until in 1832, perhaps in simple self-defense or perhaps in simple weariness, a constitution was written designating Jackson as the capital if not in perpetuity at least in escrow until 1850, when (hoped perhaps) a maturer legislature would be composed of maturer men outgrown or anyway become used to the novelty of manipulation;

Which by that time was enough; Jackson was secure, impregnable to simple toyment; fixed and founded strong, it would endure always; men had come there to live and the railroads had followed them, crossing off with steel cancellations the age of the steamboat: in '36 to Vicksburg, in '37 to Natchez, then last of all the junction of two giving a route from New Orleans to Tennessee and the Southern railroad to New York and the Atlantic ocean; secure and fixed: in 1836 Old Hickory himself addressed the legislature in its own halls, five years later Henry Clay was entertained under that roof; it knew the convention called to consider Clay's last compromise, it saw that Convention in 1861 which declared Mississippi to be the third star in that new galaxy of commonwealths dedicated to the principle that voluntary communities of men shall be not just safe but even secured from Federal meddling, and knew General Pemberton while defending that principle and right, and Joseph Johnston: and Sherman: and fire: and nothing remained, a City of Chimneys (once pigs rooted in the streets; now rats did) ruled over by a general of the

United States army while the new blood poured in: men who had followed, pressed close the Federal field armies with spoiled grain and tainted meat and spavined mules, now pressing close the Federal provost-marshals with carpet bags stuffed with blank ballot-forms on which freed slaves could mark their formal X's;

But endured; the government, which fled before Sherman in 1863, returned in '65, and even grew too despite the fact that a city government of carpet-baggers held on long after the State as a whole had dispossessed them; in 1869 Tougaloo College for Negroes was founded, in 1884 Jackson College for Negroes was brought from Natchez, in 1898 Campbell College for Negroes removed from Vicksburg; Negro leaders developed by these schools intervened when in 1868 one 'Buzzard' Egglestone instigated the use of troops to drive Governor Humphries from the executive offices and mansion; in 1887 Jackson women sponsored the Kermis Ball lasting three days to raise money for a monument to the Confederate dead; in 1884 Jefferson Davis spoke for his last time in public at the old Capitol; in 1890 the state's greatest convention drew up the present constitution;

And still the people and the railroads: the New Orleans and Great Northern down the Pearl River valley, the Gulf Mobile and Northern northeast; Alabama and the eastern black prairies were almost a commuter's leap and a line to Yazoo City and the upper river towns made of the Great Lakes five suburban ponds; the Gulf and Ship Island opened the south Mississippi lumber boom and Chicago voices spoke among the magnolias and the odor of jasmine and oleander; population doubled and trebled in a decade, in 1892 Millsaps College opened its doors to assume its place among the first establishments for higher learning; then the natural gas and the oil, Texas and Oklahoma license plates flitted like a migration of birds about the land and the tall flames from the vent-pipes stood like incandescent plumes above the century-cold ashes of Choctaw camp-fires and the vanished imprints of deer; and in 1903 the new Capitol was completed—the golden dome, the knob, the gleamy crumb, the gilded pustule longer than the miasma and the gigantic ephemeral saurians, more durable than the ice and the pre-night cold, soaring, hanging as one blinding spheroid above the center of the Commonwealth, incapable of being either looked full or evaded, peremptory, irrefragible, and reassuring;

In the roster of Mississippi names:
Claiborne. Humphries. Dickson. McLaurin. Barksdale. Lamar. Prentiss. Davis. Sartoris. Compson;

In the roster of cities:
JACKSON. Alt. 294 ft. Pop. (A.D.1950) 201,092.
Railroads: Illinois Central, Yazoo & Mississippi Valley, Alabama & Vicksburg, Gulf & Ship Island.
Bus: Tri-State Transit, Vanardo, Thomas, Greyhound,

Dixie-Greyhound, Teche-Greyhound, Oliver.

Air: Delta, Chicago & Southern.

Transport: Street buses, Taxis.

Accommodations: Hotels, Tourist camps, Rooming houses.

Radio: WJDX, WTJS.

Diversions: chronic: S.I.A.A., Basketball Tournament, Music Festival, Junior Auxiliary Follies, May Day Festival, State Tennis Tournament, Red Cross Water Pageant, State Fair, Junior Auxiliary Style Show, Girl Scouts Horse Show, Feast of Carols.

Diversions: acute: Religion, Politics.

Office of the Governor of the State. 2:00 A.M. March
twelfth.

The whole bottom of the stage is in darkness, as in Scene
I, Act One, so that the visible scene has the effect of being
held in the beam of a spotlight. Suspended too, since it
is upper left and even higher above the shadow of the
stage proper than the same in Scene I, Act One, carrying
still further the symbolism of the still higher, the last,
the ultimate seat of judgment.

It is a corner or section of the office of the Governor of
the Commonwealth, late at night, about two A.M.—a
clock on the wall says two minutes past two—, a massive
flat-topped desk bare except for an ashtray and a telephone, behind it a high-backed heavy chair like a throne;
on the wall behind and above the chair, is the emblem,
official badge, of the State, sovereignty (a mythical one,
since this is rather the State of which Yoknapatawpha
County is a unit)—an eagle, the blind scales of justice,
a device in Latin perhaps, against a flag. There are two
other chairs in front of the desk, turned slightly to face
each other, the length of the desk between them.

The Governor stands in front of the high chair, between
it and the desk, beneath the emblem on the wall. He is
symbolic too: no known person, neither old nor young;

he might be someone's idea not of God but of Gabriel perhaps, the Gabriel not before the Crucifixion but after it. He has obviously just been routed out of bed or at least out of his study or dressing-room; he wears a dressing gown, though there is a collar and tie beneath it, and his hair is neatly combed.

Temple and Stevens have just entered. Temple wears the same fur coat, hat, bag, gloves etc. as in Act One, Scene II, Stevens is dressed exactly as he was in Scene III, Act One, is carrying his hat. They are moving toward the two chairs at either end of the desk.

STEVENS

Good morning, Henry. Here we are.

GOVERNOR

Yes. Sit down.

> (as Temple sits down)

Does Mrs Stevens smoke?

STEVENS

Yes. Thank you.

He takes a pack of cigarettes from his topcoat pocket, as though he had come prepared for the need, emergency. He works one of them free and extends the pack to Temple. The Governor puts one hand into his dressing-gown pocket and withdraws it, holding something in his closed fist.

> TEMPLE
>> (takes the cigarette)

What, no blindfold?

>> (the Governor extends his hand across the desk. It contains a lighter. Temple puts the cigarette into her mouth. The Governor snaps on the lighter)

But of course, the only one waiting execution is back there in Jefferson. So all we need to do here is fire away, and hope that at least the volley rids us of the metaphor.

> GOVERNOR

Metaphor?

> TEMPLE

The blindfold. The firing squad. Or is metaphor wrong? Or maybe it's the joke. But dont apologise; a joke that has to be diagrammed is like trying to excuse an egg, isn't it? The only thing you can do is, bury them both, quick.

>> (the Governor approaches the flame to Temple's cigarette. She leans and accepts the light, then sits back)

Thanks.

The Governor closes the lighter, sits down in the tall chair behind the desk, still holding the lighter in his hand, his hands resting on the desk before him. Stevens sits down in the other chair across from Temple, laying the pack of cigarettes on the desk beside him.

GOVERNOR

What has Mrs Gowan Stevens to tell me?

TEMPLE

Not tell you: ask you. No, that's wrong. I could have asked you to revoke or commute or whatever you do to a sentence to hang when we— Uncle Gavin telephoned you last night.

(to Stevens)

Go on. Tell him. Aren't you the mouthpiece?— isn't that how you say it? Don't lawyers always tell their patients—I mean clients—never to say anything at all: to let them do all the talking?

GOVERNOR

That's only before the client enters the witness stand.

TEMPLE

So this is the witness stand.

GOVERNOR

You have come all the way here from Jefferson

at two o'clock in the morning. What would you call it?

TEMPLE

All right. *Touché* then. But not Mrs Gowan Stevens: Temple Drake. You remember Temple: the all-Mississippi debutante whose finishing school was the Memphis sporting house? About eight years ago, remember? Not that anyone, certainly not the sovereign state of Mississippi's first paid servant, need be reminded of that, provided they could read newspapers eight years ago or were kin to somebody who could read eight years ago or even had a friend who could or even just hear or even just remember or just believe the worst or even just hope for it.

GOVERNOR

I think I remember. What has Temple Drake to tell me then?

TEMPLE

That's not first. The first thing is, how much will I have to tell? I mean, how much of it that you don't already know, so that I won't be wasting all of our times telling it over? It's two o'clock in the morning; you want to—maybe even need to—sleep some, even if you are our first paid

servant; maybe even because of that— You see?
I'm already lying. What does it matter to me
how much sleep the state's first paid servant loses,
any more than it matters to the first paid servant,
a part of whose job is being paid to lose sleep
over the Nancy Mannigoes and Temple Drakes?

STEVENS

Not lying.

TEMPLE

All right. Stalling, then. So maybe if his excellency or his honor or whatever they call him, will
answer the question, we can get on.

STEVENS

Why not let the question go, and just get on?

GOVERNOR

(to Temple)

Ask me your question. How much of what do I
already know?

TEMPLE

(after a moment: she doesn't
answer at first, staring at the
Governor: then:)

Uncle Gavin's right. Maybe you are the one to
ask the questions. Only, make it as painless as
possible. Because it's going to be a little . . .

painful, to put it euphoniously—at least 'euphonious' is right, isn't it?—no matter who bragged about blindfolds.

GOVERNOR

Tell me about Nancy—Mannihoe, Mannikoe—how does she spell it?

TEMPLE

She doesn't. She can't. She can't read or write either. You are hanging her under Mannigoe, which may be wrong too, though after tomorrow morning it won't matter.

GOVERNOR

Oh yes, Manigault. The old Charleston name.

STEVENS

Older than that. Maingault. Nancy's heritage—or anyway her patronym—runs Norman blood.

GOVERNOR

Why not start by telling me about her?

TEMPLE

You are so wise. She was a dopefiend whore that my husband and I took out of the gutter to nurse our children. She murdered one of them and is to be hung tomorrow morning. We—her lawyer and I—have come to ask you to save her.

GOVERNOR

Yes. I know all that. Why?

TEMPLE

Why am I, the mother whose child she murdered, asking you to save her? Because I have forgiven her.

> (the Governor watches her, he and Stevens both do, waiting. She stares back at the Governor steadily, not defiant: just alert)

Because she was crazy.

> (the Governor watches her: she stares back, puffing rapidly at the cigarette)

All right. You don't mean why I am asking you to save her, but why I—we hired a whore and a tramp and a dopefiend to nurse our children.

> (she puffs rapidly, talking through the smoke)

To give her another chance—a human being too, even a nigger dopefiend whore—

STEVENS

Nor that, either.

TEMPLE

> (rapidly, with a sort of despair)

Oh yes, not even stalling now. Why can't you stop lying? You know: just stop for a while or a time like you can stop playing tennis or running or dancing or drinking or eating sweets during Lent. You know: not to reform: just to quit for a while, clear your system, rest up for a new tune or set or lie? All right. It was to have someone to talk to. And now you see? I'll have to tell the rest of it in order to tell you why I had to have a dopefiend whore to talk to, why Temple Drake, the white woman, the all-Mississippi debutante, descendant of long lines of statesmen and soldiers high and proud in the high proud annals of our sovereign state, couldn't find anybody except a nigger dopefiend whore that could speak her language—

GOVERNOR

Yes. This far, this late at night. Tell it.

TEMPLE

(she puffs rapidly at the cigarette, leans and crushes it out in the ashtray and sits erect again. She speaks in a hard rapid brittle emotionless voice)

Whore, dopefiend; hopeless, already damned before she was ever born, whose only reason for

living was to get the chance to die a murderess on the gallows.—Who not only entered
the home of the socialite Gowan Stevenses out
of the gutter, but made her debut into the
public life of her native city while lying in the
gutter with a white man trying to kick her teeth
or at least her voice back down her throat.—You
remember, Gavin: what was his name? it was
before my time in Jefferson, but you remember:
the cashier in the bank, the pillar of the church
or anyway in the name of his childless wife; and
this Monday morning and still drunk, Nancy
comes up while he is unlocking the front door of
the bank and fifty people standing at his back to
get in, and Nancy comes into the crowd and right
up to him and says, 'Where's my two dollars,
white man?' and he turned and struck her,
knocked her across the pavement into the gutter
and then ran after her, stomping and kicking at
her face or anyway her voice which was still saying 'Where's my two dollars, white man?' until
the crowd caught and held him still kicking at
the face lying in the gutter, spitting blood and
teeth and still saying, 'It was two dollars more
than two weeks ago and you done been back twice
since'—

She stops speaking, presses both hands to her face for
an instant, then removes them.

TEMPLE

No, no handkerchief; Lawyer Stevens and I made
a dry run on handkerchiefs before we left home
tonight. Where was I?

GOVERNOR
(quotes her)
'It was already two dollars'—

TEMPLE

So now I've got to tell all of it. Because that was
just Nancy Mannigoe. Temple Drake was in more
than just a two-dollar Saturday-night house. But
then, I said *touché*, didn't I?

She leans forward and starts to take up the crushed
cigarette from the ashtray. Stevens picks up the pack
from the desk and prepares to offer it to her. She withdraws her hand from the crushed cigarette and sits back.

TEMPLE
(to the proffered cigarette in
Stevens' hand)
No, thanks; I wont need it, after all. From here
out, it's merely anticlimax. *Coup de grace.* The
victim never feels that, does he?—Where was I?
(quickly)
Never mind. I said that before too, didn't I?
(she sits for a moment, her

(hands gripped in her lap,
motionless)
There seems to be some of this, quite a lot of this,
which even our first paid servant is not up on;
maybe because he has been our first paid servant
for less than two years yet. Though that's wrong
too; he could read eight years ago, couldn't he?
In fact, he couldn't have been elected Governor
of even Mississippi if he hadn't been able to read
at least three years in advance, could he?

STEVENS

Temple.

TEMPLE

(to Stevens)
Why not? It's just stalling, isn't it?

GOVERNOR

(watching Temple)
Hush, Gavin.
(to Temple)
Coup de grace not only means mercy, but is.
Deliver it. Give her the cigarette, Gavin.

TEMPLE

(sits forward again)
No, thanks. Really.
(after a second)

Sorry.

(quickly)

You'll notice, I always remember to say that, always remember my manners,—'raising' as we put it. Showing that I really sprang from gentle-folks, not Norman knights like Nancy did, but at least people who dont insult the host in his own house, especially at two oclock in the morning. Only, I just sprang too far, where Nancy merely stumbled modestly: a lady again, you see.

(after a moment)

There again. I'm not even stalling now: I'm fault-ing—what do they call it? burking. You know: here we are at the fence again; we've got to jump it this time, or crash. You know: slack the snaffle, let her mouth it a little, take hold, a light hold, just enough to have something to jump against; then touch her. So here we are, right back where we started, and so we can start over. So how much will I have to tell, say, speak out loud so that anybody with ears can hear it, about Temple Drake that I never thought that anything on earth, least of all the murder of my child and the execution of a nigger dopefiend whore, would ever make me tell? That I came here at two o'clock in the morning to wake you up to listen to, after eight years of being safe or at least quiet? You know: how much will I have to tell, to make it good and painful of course, but quick too, so

that you can revoke or commute the sentence or
whatever you do to it, and we can all go back
home to sleep or at least to bed? Painful of
course, but just painful enough—I think you said
'euphoniously' was right, didn't you?

GOVERNOR

Death is painful. A shameful one, even more so
—which is not too euphonious, even at best.

TEMPLE

Oh, death. We're not talking about death now.
We're talking about shame. Nancy Mannigoe has
no shame; all she has is, to die. But *touché* for
me too; haven't I brought Temple Drake all the
way here at two o'clock in the morning for the
reason that all Nancy Mannigoe has, is to die?

STEVENS

Tell him, then.

TEMPLE

He hasn't answered my question yet.
> (to Governor)

Try to answer it. How much will I have to tell?
Don't just say 'everything'. I've already heard
that.

GOVERNOR

I know who Temple Drake was: the young woman student at the University eight years ago who left the school one morning on a special train of students to attend a baseball game at another college, and disappeared from the train somewhere during its run, and vanished, nobody knew where, until she reappeared six weeks later as a witness in a murder trial in Jefferson, produced by the lawyer of the man who, it was then learned, had abducted her and held her pris-oner—

TEMPLE

—in the Memphis sporting house: don't forget that.

GOVERNOR

—in order to produce her to prove his alibi in the murder—

TEMPLE

—that Temple Drake knew had done the murder for the very good reason that—

STEVENS

Wait. Let me play too. She got off the train at the instigation of a young man who met the train at an intermediate stop with an automobile, the plan being to drive on to the ball game in the car, except that the young man was drunk at the time and got drunker, and wrecked the car and stranded both of them at the moonshiner's house where the murder happened, and from which the murderer kidnapped her and carried her to Memphis, to hold her until he would need his alibi. Afterward he—the young man with the automobile, her escort and protector at the moment of the abduction—married her. He is her husband now. He is my nephew.

TEMPLE
(to Stevens, bitterly)
You too. So wise too. Why can't you believe in truth? At least that I'm trying to tell it. At least trying now to tell it.
(to Governor)
Where was I?

GOVERNOR
(quotes)
That Temple Drake knew had done the murder for the very good reason that—

TEMPLE
Oh yes. —for the very good reason that she saw him do it, or at least his shadow: and so produced by his lawyer in the Jefferson courtroom

so that she could swear away the life of the man who was accused of it. Oh yes, that's the one. And now I've already told you something you nor nobody else but the Memphis lawyer knew, and I haven't even started. You see? I can't even bargain with you. You haven't even said yes or no yet, whether you can save her or not, whether you want to save her or not, will consider saving her or not; which, if either of us, Temple Drake or Mrs Gowan Stevens either, had any sense, would have demanded first of you.

GOVERNOR

Do you want to ask me that first?

TEMPLE

I can't. I don't dare. You might say no.

GOVERNOR

Then you wouldn't have to tell me about Temple Drake.

TEMPLE

I've got to do that. I've got to say it all, or I wouldn't be here. But unless I can still believe that you might say yes, I don't see how I can. Which is another *touché* for somebody: God, maybe—if there is one. You see? That's what's so terrible. We don't even need Him. Simple evil

is enough. Even after eight years, it's still enough.
It was eight years ago that Uncle Gavin said—oh
yes, he was there too; didn't you just hear him?
He could have told you all of this or anyway most
of it over the telephone and you could be in
bed asleep right this minute—said how there
is a corruption even in just looking at evil, even
by accident; that you can't haggle, traffic, with
putrefaction—you can't, you don't dare—

> (she stops, tense, motion-
> less)

GOVERNOR

Take the cigarette now.

> (to Stevens)

Gavin—

> (Stevens takes up the pack
> and prepares to offer the
> cigarette)

TEMPLE

No, thanks. It's too late now. Because here we
go. If we can't jump the fence, we can at least
break through it—

STEVENS

> (interrupts)

Which means that anyway one of us will get over
standing up.

(as Temple reacts)

Oh yes, I'm still playing; I'm going to ride this one too. Go ahead.

(prompting)

Temple Drake—

TEMPLE

—Temple Drake, the foolish virgin; that is, a virgin as far as anybody went on record to disprove, but a fool certainly by anybody's standards and computation; seventeen, and more of a fool than simply being a virgin or even being seventeen could excuse or account for; indeed, showing herself capable of a height of folly which even seven or three, let alone mere virginity, could scarcely have matched—

STEVENS

Give the brute a chance. Try at least to ride him at the fence and not just through it.

TEMPLE

You mean the Virginia gentleman.

(to Governor)

That's my husband. He went to the University of Virginia, trained, Uncle Gavin would say, at Virginia not only in drinking but in gentility too—

STEVENS

—and ran out of both at the same instant that day eight years ago when he took her off the train and wrecked the car at the moonshiner's house.

TEMPLE

But relapsed into one of them at least because at least he married me as soon as he could.
(to Stevens)
You don't mind my telling his excellency that, do you?

STEVENS

A relapse into both of them. He hasn't had a drink since that day either. His excellency might bear that in mind too.

GOVERNOR

I will. I have.

(he makes just enough of a pause to cause them both to stop and look at him)

I almost wish—

(they are both watching him; this is the first intimation we have that something is going on here, an undercurrent: that the Governor

and Stevens know something
which Temple doesn't: to
Temple)

He didn't come with you.

STEVENS
(mildly yet quickly)
Won't there be time for that later, Henry?

TEMPLE
(quick, defiant, suspicious,
hard)

Who didn't?

GOVERNOR

Your husband.

TEMPLE
(quick and hard)

Why?

GOVERNOR

You have come here to plead for the life of the
murderess of your child. Your husband was its
parent too.

TEMPLE

You're wrong. We didn't come here at two
o'clock in the morning to save Nancy Mannigoe.
Nancy Mannigoe is not even concerned in this

because Nancy Mannigoe's lawyer told me before we ever left Jefferson that you were not
going to save Nancy Mannigoe. What we came
here and waked you up at two o'clock in the
morning for is just to give Temple Drake a good
fair honest chance to suffer—you know: just anguish for the sake of anguish, like that Russian
or somebody who wrote a whole book about
suffering, not suffering for or about anything,
just suffering, like somebody unconscious not
really breathing for anything but just breathing.
Or maybe that's wrong too and nobody really
cares, suffers, any more about suffering than they
do about truth or justice or Temple Drake's
shame or Nancy Mannigoe's worthless nigger
life—

She stops speaking, sitting quite still, erect in the chair,
her face raised slightly, not looking at either of them
while they watch her.

GOVERNOR
Give her the handkerchief now.

Stevens takes a fresh handkerchief from his pocket,
shakes it out and extends it toward Temple. She does not
move, her hands still clasped in her lap. Stevens rises,
crosses, drops the handkerchief into her lap, returns to
his chair.

TEMPLE

Thanks really. But it doesn't matter now; we're too near the end; you could almost go on down to the car and start it and have the engine warming up while I finish.

(to Governor)

You see? All you'll have to do now is just be still and listen. Or not even listen if you dont want to: but just be still, just wait. And not long either now, and then we can all go to bed and turn off the light. And then, night: dark: sleep even maybe, when with the same arm you turn off the light and pull the covers up with, you can put away forever Temple Drake and whatever it is you have done about her, and Nancy Mannigoe and whatever it is you have done about her, if you're going to do anything, if it even matters anyhow whether you do anything or not, and none of it will ever have to bother us any more. Because Uncle Gavin was only partly right. It's not that you must never even look on evil and corruption; sometimes you can't help that, you are not always warned. It's not even that you must resist it always. Because you've got to start much sooner than that. You've got to be already prepared to resist it, say no to it, long before you see it; you must have already said no to it long before you even know what it is. I'll have the cigarette now, please.

Stevens takes up the pack, rising and working the end of a cigarette free, and extends the pack. She takes the cigarette, already speaking again while Stevens puts the pack on the desk and takes up the lighter which the Governor, watching Temple, shoves across the desk where Stevens can reach it. Stevens snaps the lighter on and holds it out. Temple makes no effort to light the cigarette, holding the cigarette in her hand and talking. Then she lays the cigarette unlighted on the ashtray and Stevens closes the lighter and sits down again, putting the lighter down beside the pack of cigarettes.

TEMPLE
Because Temple Drake liked evil. She only went to the ball game because she would have to get on a train to do it, so that she could slip off the train the first time it stopped, and get into the car to drive a hundred miles with a man—

STEVENS
—who couldn't hold his drink.

TEMPLE
(to Stevens)
All right. Aren't I just saying that?
(to Governor)
An optimist. Not the young man; he was just doing the best he knew, could. It wasn't him that suggested the trip: it was Temple—

STEVENS

It was his car though. Or his mother's.

TEMPLE

(to Stevens)

All right. All right.

(to Governor)

No, Temple was the optimist: not that she had foreseen, planned ahead either: she just had unbounded faith that her father and brothers would know evil when they saw it, so all she had to do was, do the one thing which she knew they would forbid her to do if they had the chance. And they were right about the evil, and so of course she was right too, though even then it was not easy: she even had to drive the car for a while after we began to realize that the young man was wrong, had graduated too soon in the drinking part of his Virginia training—

STEVENS

It was Gowan who knew the moonshiner and insisted on going there.

TEMPLE

—and even then—

STEVENS

He was driving when you wrecked.

TEMPLE

> (to Stevens: quick and
> harsh)

And married me for it. Does he have to pay for
it twice? It wasn't really worth paying for once,
was it?

> (to Governor)

And even then—

GOVERNOR

How much was it worth?

TEMPLE

Was what worth?

GOVERNOR

His marrying you.

TEMPLE

You mean to him, of course. Less than he paid
for it.

GOVERNOR

Is that what he thinks too?

> (they stare at one another,
> Temple alert, quite watch-
> ful, though rather impatient
> than anything else)

You're going to tell me something that he doesn't know, else you would have brought him with you. Is that right?

TEMPLE

Yes.

GOVERNOR

Would you tell it if he were here?

> (Temple is staring at the Governor. Unnoticed by her, Stevens makes a faint movement. The Governor stops him with a slight motion of one hand which also Temple does not notice)

Now that you have come this far, now that, as you said, you have got to tell it, say it aloud, not to save Nan—this woman, but because you decided before you left home tonight that there is nothing else to do but tell it.

TEMPLE

How do I know whether I would or not?

GOVERNOR

Suppose he was here—sitting in that chair where Gav—your uncle is—

TEMPLE

—or behind the door or in one of your desk
drawers, maybe? He's not. He's at home. I gave
him a sleeping pill.

GOVERNOR

But suppose he was, now that you have got to say
it. Would you still say it?

TEMPLE

All right. Yes. Now will you please shut up too
and let me tell it? How can I, if you and Gavin
won't hush and let me? I can't even remember
where I was.—Oh yes. So I saw the murder, or
anyway the shadow of it, and the man took me to
Memphis, and I know that too, I had two legs and
I could see, and I could have simply screamed up
the main street of any of the little towns we
passed, just as I could have walked away from
the car after Gow—we ran it into the tree, and
stopped a wagon or a car which would have
carried me to the nearest town or railroad station
or even back to school or, for that matter, right
on back home into my father's or brothers' hands.
But not me, not Temple. I choose the murderer—

STEVENS

(to Governor)

He was a psychopath, though that didn't come out

in the trial, and when it did come out, or could have come out, it was too late. I was there; I saw that too: a little black thing with an Italian name, like a neat and only slightly deformed cockroach: a hybrid, sexually incapable. But then, she will tell you that too.

TEMPLE
> (with bitter sarcasm)

Dear Uncle Gavin.

> (to Governor)

Oh yes, that too, her bad luck too: to plump for a thing which didn't even have sex for his weakness, but just murder—

> (she stops, sitting motionless, erect, her h a n d s clenched on her lap, her eyes closed)

If you both would just hush, just let me. I seem to be like trying to drive a hen into a barrel. Maybe if you would just try to act like you wanted to keep her out of it, from going into it—

GOVERNOR
Don't call it a barrel. Call it a tunnel. That's a thoroughfare, because the other end is open too. Go through it. There was no—sex.

TEMPLE
Not from him. He was worse than a father or uncle. It was worse than being the wealthy ward

of the most indulgent trust or insurance company:
carried to Memphis and shut up in that Manuel
Street sporting house like a ten-year-old bride
in a Spanish convent, with the madam herself
more eagle-eyed than any mama—and the Negro
maid to guard the door while the madam would
be out, to wherever she would go, wherever the
madams of cat houses go on their afternoons
out, to pay police-court fines or protection or
to the bank or maybe just visiting, which would
not be so bad because the maid would unlock the
door and come inside and we could—

(she falters, pauses for less
than a second; then quickly)

Yes, that's why—talk. A prisoner of course, and
maybe not in a very gilded cage, but at least
the prisoner was. I had perfume by the quart;
some salesgirl chose it of course, and it was the
wrong kind, but at least I had it, and he bought
me a fur coat—with nowhere to wear it of
course because he wouldn't let me out, but I
had the coat—and snazzy underwear and
negligees, selected also by salesgirls but at
least the best or anyway the most expensive—
the taste at least of the big end of an underworld big shot's wallet. Because he wanted me
to be contented, you see; and not only contented,
he didn't even mind if I was happy too: just
so I was there when or in case the police finally

connected him with that Mississippi murder;
not only didn't mind if I was happy; he even
made the effort himself to see that I was. And so
at last we have come to it, because now I have
got to tell you this too to give you a valid
reason why I waked you up at two in the
morning to ask you to save a murderess.

She stops speaking, reaches and takes the unlighted cigarette from the tray, then realises it is unlit. Stevens
takes up the lighter from the desk and starts to get up.
Still watching Temple, the Governor makes to Stevens a
slight arresting signal with his hand. Stevens pauses,
then pushes the lighter along the desk to where Temple
can reach it, and sits back down. Temple takes the lighter,
snaps it on, lights the cigarette, closes the lighter and
puts it back on the desk. But after only one puff at the
cigarette, she lays it back on the tray and sits again as
before, speaking again.

TEMPLE

Because I still had the two arms and legs and
eyes; I could have climbed down the rainspout
at any time, the only difference being that I
didn't. I would never leave the room except late
at night, when he would come in a closed car
the size of an undertaker's wagon, and he and
the chauffeur on the front seat, and me and the
madam in the back, rushing at forty and fifty

and sixty miles an hour up and down the back
alleys of the redlight district. Which—the back
alleys—was all I ever saw of them too. I was
not even permitted to meet or visit with or even
see the other girls in my own house, not even
to sit with them after work and listen to the
shop talk while they counted their chips or
blisters or whatever they would do sitting on one
another's beds in the elected dormitory. . . .

> (she pauses again, continues
> in a sort of surprise, amaze-
> ment)

Yes, it was like the dormitory at school: the
smell: of women, young women all busy thinking not about men but just man: only a little
stronger, a little calmer, less excited—sitting
on the temporarily idle beds discussing the
exigencies—that's surely the right one, isn't it?
—of their trade. But not me, not Temple: shut
up in that room twenty-four hours a day, with
nothing to do but hold fashion shows in the
fur coat and the flashy pants and negligees, with
nothing to see it but a two-foot mirror and a
Negro maid; hanging bone dry and safe in the
middle of sin and pleasure like being suspended
twenty fathoms deep in an ocean diving bell.
Because he wanted her to be contented, you
see. He even made the last effort himself. But
Temple didn't want to be just contented. So she

had to do what us sporting girls call fall in
love.

GOVERNOR

Ah.

STEVENS

That's right.

TEMPLE
>   (quickly: to Stevens)

Hush.

STEVENS
>   (to Temple)

Hush yourself.
>   (to Governor)

He—Vitelli—they called him Popeye—brought
the man there himself. He—the young man—.

TEMPLE

Gavin! No, I tell you!

STEVENS
>   (to Temple)

You are drowning in an orgasm of abjectness
and moderation when all you need is truth.
>   (to Governor)

—was known in his own circles as Red, Alabama
Red; not to the police, or not officially, since he

was not a criminal, or anyway not yet, but just a thug, probably cursed more by simple eupepsia than by anything else. He was a houseman—the bouncer—at the nightclub, joint, on the outskirts of town, which Popeye owned and which was Popeye's headquarters. He died shortly afterward in the alley behind Temple's prison, of a bullet from the same pistol which had done the Mississippi murder, though Popeye too was dead, hanged in Alabama for a murder he did not commit, before the pistol was ever found and connected with him.

GOVERNOR

I see. This—Popeye—

STEVENS

—discovered himself betrayed by one of his own servants, and took a princely vengeance on his honor's smircher? You will be wrong. You underrate this *precieux*, this flower, this jewel. Vitelli. What a name for him. A hybrid, impotent. He was hanged the next year, to be sure. But even that was wrong: his very effacement debasing, flouting, even what dignity man has been able to lend to necessary human abolishment. He should have been crushed somehow under a vast and mindless boot, like a spider. He didn't sell her; you violate and outrage his very memory with that crass and material impugnment. He was a purist, an amateur always: he did not even murder for base profit. It was not even for simple lust. He was a gourmet, a sybarite, centuries, perhaps hemispheres before his time; in spirit and glands he was of that age of princely despots to whom the ability even to read was vulgar and plebeian and, reclining on silk amid silken airs and scents, had eunuch slaves for that office, commanding death to the slave at the end of each reading, each evening, that none else alive, even a eunuch slave, shall have shared in, partaken of, remembered, the poem's evocation.

GOVERNOR

I dont think I understand.

STEVENS

Try to. Uncheck your capacity for rage and re-vulsion—the sort of rage and revulsion it takes to step on a worm. If Vitelli cannot evoke that in you, his life will have been indeed a desert.

TEMPLE

Or don't try to. Just let it go. Just for God's sake let it go. I met the man, how doesn't matter, and I fell what I called in love with him and what it was or what I called it doesn't matter

either because all that matters is that I wrote
the letters—

GOVERNOR

I see. This is the part that her husband didn't
know.

TEMPLE
(to Governor)

And what does that matter either? Whether he
knows or not? What can another face or two or
name or two matter, since he knows that I lived
for six weeks in a Manuel Street brothel? Or
another body or two in the bed? Or three or
four? I'm trying to tell it, enough of it. Can't
you see that? But can't you make him let me
alone so I can. Make him, for God's sake, let
me alone.

GOVERNOR
(to Stevens: watching Temple)

No more, Gavin.
(to Temple)

So you fell in love.

TEMPLE

Thank you for that. I mean, the 'love.' Except
that I didn't even fall, I was already there: the

bad, the lost: who could have climbed down
the gutter or lightning rod any time and got
away, or even simpler than that: disguised myself as the nigger maid with a stack of towels
and a bottle opener and change for ten dollars,
and walked right out the front door. So I wrote
the letters. I would write one each time . . .
afterward, after they—he left, and sometimes I
would write two or three when it would be two
or three days between, when they—he wouldn't—

GOVERNOR

What? What's that?

TEMPLE

—you know: something to do, be doing, filling
the time, better than the fashion parades in
front of the two-foot glass with nobody to be
disturbed even by the . . . pants, or even no
pants. Good letters—

GOVERNOR

Wait. What did you say?

TEMPLE

I said they were good letters, even for—

GOVERNOR

You said, after *they* left.

(they look at one another.
Temple doesn't answer: to
Stevens, though still watch-
ing Temple)
Am I being told that this . . . Vitelli would be
there in the room too?

STEVENS

Yes. That was why he brought him. You can see
now what I meant by connoisseur and gourmet.

GOVERNOR

And what you meant by the boot too. But he's
dead. You know that.

STEVENS

Oh yes. He's dead. And I said 'purist' too. To the
last: hanged the next summer in Alabama for a
murder he didn't even commit and which nobody involved in the matter really believed he
had committed, only not even his lawyer could
persuade him to admit that he couldn't have done
it if he had wanted to, or wouldn't have done it if
the notion had struck him. Oh yes, he's dead too;
we haven't come here for vengeance.

GOVERNOR

(to Temple)
Yes. Go on. The letters.

TEMPLE

The letters. They were good letters. I mean—
good ones.

> (staring steadily at the Gov-
> ernor)

What I'm trying to say is, they were the kind of
letters that if you had written them to a man, even
eight years ago, you wouldn't—would—rather
your husband didn't see them, no matter what
he thought about your—past.

> (still staring at the Governor
> as she makes her painful
> confession)

Better than you would expect from a seventeen-
year-old amateur. I mean, you would have won-
dered how anybody just seventeen and not even
through freshman in college, could have learned
the—right words. Though all you would have
needed probably would be an old dictionary from
back in Shakespeare's time when, so they say,
people hadn't learned how to blush at words.
That is, anybody except Temple Drake, who
didn't need a dictionary, who was a fast learner
and so even just one lesson would have been
enough for her, let alone three or four or a dozen
or two or three dozen.

> (staring at the Governor)

No, not even one lesson because the bad was
already there waiting, who hadn't even heard yet

that you must be already resisting the corruption not only before you look at it but before you even know what it is, what you are resisting. So I wrote the letters, I don't know how many, enough, more than enough because just one would have been enough. And that's all.

GOVERNOR

All?

TEMPLE

Yes. You've certainly heard of blackmail. The letters turned up again of course. And of course, being Temple Drake, the first way to buy them back that Temple Drake thought of, was to produce the material for another set of them.

STEVENS

(to Temple)

Yes, that's all. But you've got to tell him why it's all.

TEMPLE

I thought I had. I wrote some letters that you would have thought that even Temple Drake might have been ashamed to put on paper, and then the man I wrote them to died, and I married another man and reformed, or thought I had, and bore two children and hired another reformed whore so that I would have somebody to talk to, and I even thought I had forgotten about the letters until they turned up again and then I found out that I not only hadn't forgot about the letters, I hadn't even reformed—

STEVENS

All right. Do you want me to tell it, then?

TEMPLE

And you were the one preaching moderation.

STEVENS

I was preaching against orgasms of it.

TEMPLE

(bitterly)

Oh, I know. Just suffering. Not for anything: just suffering. Just because it's good for you, like calomel or ipecac.

(to Governor)

All right. What?

GOVERNOR

The young man died—

TEMPLE

Oh yes.—Died, shot from a car while he was slipping up the alley behind the house, to climb up the same drainpipe I could have climbed

down at any time and got away, to see me—the
one time, the first time, the only time when
we thought we had dodged, fooled him, could
be alone together, just the two of us, after all
the . . . other ones.—If love can be, mean anything, except the newness, the learning, the peace,
the privacy: no shame: not even conscious that
you are naked because you are just using the
nakedness because that's a part of it; then he was
dead, killed, shot down right in the middle of
thinking about me, when in just one more minute
maybe he would have been in the room with me,
when all of him except just his body was already in the room with me and the door locked at
last for just the two of us alone; and then it
was all over and as though it had never been,
happened: it had to be as though it had never
happened, except that that was even worse—
                    (rapidly)
Then the courtroom in Jefferson and I didn't
care, not about anything any more, and my
father and brothers waiting and then the year
in Europe, Paris, and I still didn't care, and then
after a while it really did get easier. You know.
People are lucky. They are wonderful. At first
you think that you can bear only so much and
then you will be free. Then you find out that you
can bear anything, you really can and then it
won't even matter. Because suddenly it could be

as if it had never been, never happened. You
know: somebody—Hemingway, wasn't it?—
wrote a book about how it had never actually happened to a gir—woman, if she just refused to
accept it, no matter who remembered, bragged.
And besides, the ones who could—remember—
were both dead. Then Gowan came to Paris that
winter and we were married—at the Embassy,
with a reception afterward at the Crillon, and if
that couldn't fumigate an American past, what
else this side of heaven could you hope for to
remove stink? Not to mention a new automobile
and a honeymoon in a rented hideaway built for
his European mistress by a Mohammedan prince
at Cap Ferrat. Only—

> (she pauses, falters, for just
> an instant, then goes on)

—we—I thought we—I didn't want to efface the
stink really—

> (rapidly now, tense, erect,
> her hands gripped again into
> fists on her lap)

You know: just the marriage would be enough:
not the Embassy and the Crillon and Cap Ferrat
but just to kneel down, the two of us, and say 'We
have sinned, forgive us.' And then maybe there
would be the love this time—the peace, the quiet,
the no shame that I . . . didn't—missed that other
time—

> (falters again, then rapidly
> again, glib and succinct)

Love, but more than love too: not depending on
just love to hold two people together, make them
better than either one would have been alone, but
tragedy, suffering, having suffered and caused
grief; having something to have to live with even
when, because you knew both of you could never
forget it. And then I began to believe something
even more than that: that there was something
even better, stronger, than tragedy to hold two
people together: forgiveness. Only that seemed
to be wrong. Only maybe it wasn't the forgiveness
that was wrong, but the gratitude; and maybe
the only thing worse than having to give gratitude
constantly all the time, is having to accept it—

STEVENS

Which is exactly backward. What was wrong
wasn't—

GOVERNOR

Gavin.

STEVENS

Shut up yourself, Henry. What was wrong wasn't
Temple's good name. It wasn't even her husband's conscience. It was his vanity: the Virginia-
trained aristocrat caught with his gentility

around his knees like the guest in the trick Holly-
wood bathroom. So the forgiving wasn't enough
for him, or perhaps he hadn't read Hemingway's
book. Because after about a year, his restiveness
under the onus of accepting the gratitude began
to take the form of doubting the paternity of their
child.

TEMPLE

Oh God. Oh God.

GOVERNOR

Gavin.
     (Stevens stops.)
No more, I said. Call that an order.
     (to Temple)
Yes. Tell me.

TEMPLE

I'm trying to. I expected our main obstacle in
this would be the bereaved plaintiff. Apparently
though it's the defendant's lawyer. I mean, I'm
trying to tell you about one Temple Drake, and
our Uncle Gavin is showing you another one. So
already you've got two different people begging
for the same clemency; if everybody concerned
keeps on splitting up into two people, you wont
even know who to pardon, will you? And now
that I mention it, here we are, already back to

Nancy Mannigoe, and now surely it shouldn't
take long. Let's see, we'd got back to Jefferson
too, hadn't we? Anyway, we are now. I mean,
back in Jefferson, back home. You know: face it:
the disgrace: the shame, face it down, good and
down forever, never to haunt us more; together,
a common front to stink because we love each
other and have forgiven all, strong in our love
and mutual forgiveness. Besides having everything else: the Gowan Stevenses, young, popular:
a new bungalow on the right street to start the
Saturday-night hangovers in, a country club with
a country-club younger set of rallying friends to
make it a Saturday-night hangover worthy the
name of Saturday-night country-club hangover,
a pew in the right church to recover from it in,
provided of course they were not too hungover
even to get to church. Then the son and heir came;
and now we have Nancy: nurse: guide: mentor,
catalyst, glue, whatever you want to call it, holding the whole lot of them together—not just a
magnetic center for the heir apparent and the
other little princes or princesses in their orderly
succession, to circle around, but for the two
bigger hunks too of mass or matter or dirt or
whatever it is shaped in the image of God, in a
semblance at least of order and respectability
and peace; not ole cradle-rocking black mammy
at all, because the Gowan Stevenses are young

and modern, so young and modern that all the
other young country-club set applauded when
they took an ex-dopefiend nigger whore out of
the gutter to nurse their children, because the
rest of the young country-club set didn't know
that it wasn't the Gowan Stevenses but Temple
Drake who had chosen the ex-dopefiend nigger
whore for the reason that an ex-dopefiend nigger
whore was the only animal in Jefferson that
spoke Temple Drake's language—

> (quickly takes up the burn-
> ing cigarette from the tray
> and puffs at it, talking
> through the puffs)

Oh yes, I'm going to tell this too. A confidante.
You know: the big-time ball player, the idol
on the pedestal, the worshipped; and the wor-
shipper, the acolyte, the one that never had
and never would, no matter how willing or
how hard she tried, get out of the sandlots,
the bush league. You know: the long afternoons, with the last electric button pressed on the
last cooking or washing or sweeping gadget and
the baby safely asleep for a while, and the two
sisters in sin swapping trade or anyway avoca-
tional secrets over Coca-Colas in the quiet
kitchen. Somebody to talk to, as we all seem to
need, want, have to have, not to converse with
you nor even agree with you, but just keep quiet

and listen. Which is all that people really want, really need; I mean, to behave themselves, keep out of one another's hair; the maladjustments which they tell us breed the arsonists and rapists and murderers and thieves and the rest of the anti-social enemies, are not really maladjustments but simply because the embryonic murderers and thieves didn't have anybody to listen to them: which is an idea the Catholic Church discovered two thousand years ago only it just didn't carry it far enough or maybe it was too busy being the Church to have time to bother with man, or maybe it wasn't the Church's fault at all but simply because it had to deal with human beings and maybe if the world was just populated with a kind of creature half of which were dumb, couldn't do anything but listen, couldn't even escape from having to listen to the other half, there wouldn't even be any war. Which was what Temple had: somebody paid by the week just to listen, which you would have thought would have been enough; and then the other baby came, the infant, the doomed sacrifice (though of course we dont know that yet) and you would have thought that this was surely enough, that now even Temple Drake would consider herself safe, could be depended on, having two—what do sailors call them? oh yes, sheet-anchors—now. Only it wasn't enough. Because Hemingway was

right. I mean, the gir—woman in his book. All
you have got to do is, refuse to accept. Only, you
have got to . . . refuse——

STEVENS

Now, the letters——

GOVERNOR
(watching Temple)
Be quiet, Gavin.

STEVENS

No, I'm going to talk a while now. We'll even
stick to the sports metaphor and call it a relay
race, with the senior member of the team carrying the . . . baton, twig, switch, sapling, tree—
whatever you want to call the symbolical wood,
up what remains of the symbolical hill.
(the lights flicker, grow
slightly dimmer, then flare
back up and steady again, as
though in a signal, a warning)
The letters. The blackmail. The blackmailer was
Red's younger brother—a criminal of course, but
at least a man——

TEMPLE

No! No!

STEVENS

(to Temple)

Be quiet too. It only goes up a hill, not over a precipice. Besides, it's only a stick. The letters were not first. The first thing was the gratitude. And now we have even come to the husband, my nephew. And when I say 'past,' I mean that part of it which the husband knows so far, which apparently was enough in his estimation. Because it was not long before she discovered, realized, that she was going to spend a good part of the rest of her days (nights too) being forgiven for it; in being not only constantly reminded—well, maybe not specifically reminded, but say made —kept—aware of it in order to be forgiven for it so that she might be grateful to the forgiver, but in having to employ more and more of what tact she had—and the patience which she probably didn't know she had, since until now she had never occasion to need patience—to make the gratitude—in which she had probably had as little experience as she had had with patience— acceptable to meet with, match, the high standards of the forgiver. But she was not too concerned. Her husband—my nephew—had made what he probably considered the supreme sacrifice to expiate his part in her past; she had no doubts of her capacity to continue to supply whatever increasing degree of gratitude

the increasing appetite—or capacity—of its
addict would demand, in return for the sacrifice which, so she believed, she had accepted for
the same reason of gratitude. Besides, she still
had the legs and the eyes; she could walk away,
escape, from it at any moment she wished, even
though her past might have shown her that she
probably would not use the ability to locomote to
escape from threat and danger. Do you accept
that?

GOVERNOR

All right. Go on.

STEVENS

Then she discovered that the child—the first one
—was on the way. For that first instant, she must
have known something almost like frenzy. Now
she couldn't escape; she had waited too long.
But it was worse than that. It was as though she
realized for the first time that you—everyone—
must, or anyway may have to, pay for your past;
that past is something like a promissory note with
a trick clause in it which, as long as nothing goes
wrong, can be manumitted in an orderly manner,
but which fate or luck or chance, can foreclose on
you without warning. That is, she had known, accepted, this all the time and dismissed it because
she knew that she could cope, was invulnerable
through simple integration, own-womanness. But

now there would be a child, tender and defenseless. But you never really give up hope, you
know, not even after you finally realize that
people not only can bear anything, but probably
will have to, so probably even before the frenzy
had had time to fade, she found a hope: which
was the child's own tender and defenseless innocence: that God—if there was one—would protect the child—not her: she asked no quarter and
wanted none; she could cope, either cope or bear
it, but the child from the sight draft of her past—
because it was innocent, even though she knew
better, all her observation having shown her that
God either would not or could not—anyway, did
not—save innocence just because it was innocent;
that when He said 'Suffer little children to come
unto Me' He meant exactly that: He meant suffer;
that the adults, the fathers, the old in and capable
of sin, must be ready and willing—nay, eager—
to suffer at any time, that the little children shall
come unto Him unanguished, unterrified, un-
defiled. Do you accept that?

GOVERNOR

Go on.

STEVENS

So at least she had ease. Not hope: ease. It was
precarious of course, a balance, but she could
walk a tightrope too. It was as though she had

struck, not a bargain, but an armistice with God
—if there was one. She had not tried to cheat;
she had not tried to evade the promissory note of
her past by intervening the blank check of a
child's innocence—it was born now, a little boy,
a son, her husband's son and heir—between. She
had not tried to prevent the child; she had simply
never thought about pregnancy in this connection,
since it took the physical fact of the pregnancy
to reveal to her the existence of that promissory
note bearing her post-dated signature. And since
God—if there was one—must be aware of that,
then she too would bear her side of the bargain
by not demanding on Him a second time since He
—if there was one—would at least play fair,
would be at least a gentleman. And that?

GOVERNOR

Go on.

STEVENS

So you can take your choice about the second
child. Perhaps she was too busy between the three
of them to be careful enough: between the three
of them: the doom, the fate, the past; the bargain
with God; the forgiveness and the gratitude. Like
the juggler says, not with three insentient replace-
able Indian clubs or balls, but three glass bulbs
filled with nitroglycerin and not enough hands

for one even: one hand to offer the atonement
with and another to receive the forgiveness with
and a third needed to offer the gratitude, and still
a fourth hand more and more imperative as time
passed to sprinkle in steadily and constantly
increasing doses a little more and a little more
of the sugar and seasoning on the gratitude to
keep it palatable to its swallower—that perhaps:
she just didn't have time to be careful enough, or
perhaps it was desperation, or perhaps this was
when her husband first refuted or implied or
anyway impugned—whichever it was—his son's
paternity. Anyway, she was pregnant again; she
had broken her word, destroyed her talisman,
and she probably knew fifteen months before the
letters that this was the end, and when the man
appeared with the old letters she probably was
not even surprised: she had merely been wondering for fifteen months what form the doom would
take. And accept this too—

The lights flicker and dim further, then steady at that
point.

And relief too. Because at last it was over; the
roof had fallen, avalanche had roared; even the
helplessness and the impotence were finished
now, because now even the old fragility of bone
and meat was no longer a factor—and, who

knows? because of that fragility, a kind of pride, triumph: you have waited for destruction: you endured; it was inevitable, inescapable, you had no hope. Nevertheless, you did not merely cringe, crouching, your head, vision, buried in your arms; you were not watching that poised arrestment all the time, true enough, but that was not because you feared it but because you were too busy putting one foot before the other, never for one instant really flagging, faltering, even though you knew it was in vain—triumph in the very fragility which no longer need concern you now, for the reason that the all, the very worst, which catastrophe can do to you, is crush and obliterate the fragility; you were the better man, you outfaced even catastrophe, outlasted it, compelled it to move first; you did not even defy it, not even contemptuous: with no other tool or implement but that worthless fragility, you held disaster off as with one hand you might support the weightless silken canopy of a bed, for six long years while it, with all its weight and power, could not possibly prolong the obliteration of your fragility over five or six seconds; and even during that five or six seconds you would still be the better man, since all that it—the catastrophe —could deprive you of, you yourself had already written off six years ago as being, inherently of and because of its own fragile self, worthless.

GOVERNOR

And now, the man.

STEVENS

I thought you would see it too. Even the first one stuck out like a sore thumb. Yes, he—

GOVERNOR

The first what?

STEVENS

(pauses, looks at the Governor)

The first man: Red. Don't you know anything at all about women? I never saw Red or this next one, his brother, either, but all three of them, the other two and her husband, probably all look enough alike or act enough alike—maybe by simply making enough impossible unfulfillable demands on her or by being drawn to her enough to accept, risk, almost incredible conditions—to be at least first cousins. Where have you been all your life?

GOVERNOR

All right. The man.

STEVENS

At first, all he thought of, planned on, was interested in, intended, was the money—to collect for the letters, and beat it, get the hell out. Of course, even at the end, all he was really after was still the money, not only after he found out that he would have to take her and the child too to get it, but even when it looked like all he was going to get, at least for a while, was just a runaway wife and a six-months-old infant. In fact, Nancy's error, her really fatal action on that fatal and tragic night, was in not giving the money and the jewels both to him when she found where Temple had hidden them, and getting the letters and getting rid of him forever, instead of hiding the money and jewels from Temple in her turn—which was what Temple herself thought too apparently, since she—Temple —told him a lie about how much the money was, telling him it was only two hundred dollars when it was actually almost two thousand. So you would have said that he wanted the money indeed, and just how much, how badly, to have been willing to pay that price for it. Or maybe he was being wise—'smart', he would have called it—beyond his years and time, and without having actually planned it that way, was really inventing a new and safe method of kidnapping: that is, pick an adult victim capable of signing her own checks—also with an infant in arms for added persuasion—and not forcing but actually persuading her to come along under her own

power and then—still peaceably—extracting
the money later at your leisure, using the tender
welfare of the infant as a fulcrum for your lever.
Or maybe we're both wrong and both should give
credit—what little of it—where credit—what
little of it—is due, since it was just the money
with her too at first, though he was probably still
thinking it was just the money at the very time
when, having got her own jewelry together and
found where her husband kept the key to the
strongbox (and I imagine, even opened it one
night after her husband was in bed asleep and
counted the money in it or at least made sure
there was money in it or anyway that the key
would actually open it), she found herself still
trying to rationalise why she had not paid over
the money and got the letters and destroyed them
and so rid herself forever of her Damocles' roof.
Which was what she did not do. Because Hemingway—his girl—was quite right: all you have
got to do is, refuse to accept it. Only, you have
got to be told truthfully beforehand what you
must refuse; the gods owe you that—at least a
clear picture and a clear choice. Not to be fooled
by . . . who knows? probably even gentleness,
after a fashion, back there on those afternoons
or whenever they were in the Memphis . . . all
right: honeymoon, even with a witness; in this
case certainly anything much better lacked, and

indeed, who knows? (I am Red now) even a little of awe, incredulous hope, incredulous amazement, even a little of trembling at this much fortune, this much luck dropping out of the very sky itself, into his embrace; at least (Temple now) no gang: even rape become tender: only one, an individual, still refusable, giving her at least (this time) the similitude of being wooed, of an opportunity to say Yes first, letting her even believe she could say either one of yes or no. I imagine that he (the new one, the blackmailer) even looked like his brother—a younger Red, the Red of a few years even before she knew him, and—if you will permit it —less stained, so that in a way it may have seemed to her that here at last even she might slough away the six years' soilure of struggle and repentance and terror to no avail. And if this is what you meant, then you are right too: a man, at least a man, after six years of that sort of forgiving which debased not only the forgiven but the forgiven's gratitude too—a bad man of course, a criminal by intent regardless of how cramped his opportunities may have been up to this moment; and, capable of blackmail, vicious and not merely competent to, but destined to, bring nothing but evil and disaster and ruin to anyone foolish enough to enter his orbit, cast her lot with his. But—by comparison, that six years of comparison—at least a man—a man so single, so hard and ruthless, so impeccable in amorality, as to have a kind of integrity, purity, who would not only never need nor intend to forgive anyone anything, he would never even realise that anyone expected him to forgive anyone anything; who wouldn't even bother to forgive her if it ever dawned on him that he had the opportunity, but instead would simply black her eyes and knock a few teeth out and fling her into the gutter: so that she could rest secure forever in the knowledge that, until she found herself with a black eye and or spitting teeth in the gutter, he would never even know he had anything to forgive her for.

This time, the lights do not flicker. They begin to dim steadily toward and then into complete darkness as Stevens continues.

Nancy was the confidante, at first, while she— Nancy—still believed probably that the only problem, factor, was how to raise the money the blackmailer demanded, without letting the boss, the master, the husband find out about it; finding, discovering—this is still Nancy—realising probably that she had not really been a confidante for a good while, a long while before she discovered that what she actually was, was a spy:

on her employer: not realising until after she
had discovered that, although Temple had taken
the money and the jewels too from her husband's
strongbox, she—Temple—still hadn't paid them
over to the blackmailer and got the letters, that
the payment of the money and jewels was less
than half of Temple's plan.

The lights go completely out. The stage is in complete
darkness. Stevens' voice continues.

That was when Nancy in her turn found where
Temple had hidden the money and jewels, and
—Nancy—took them in her turn and hid them
from Temple; this was the night of the day
Gowan left for a week's fishing at Aransas Pass,
taking the older child, the boy, with him, to leave
the child for a week's visit with its grandparents
in New Orleans until Gowan would pick him up
on his way home from Texas.

> (to Temple: in the dark-
> ness)

Now tell him.

The stage is in complete darkness.

Interior, Temple's private sitting- or dressing-room. 9:30
P.M. September thirteenth *ante.*

The lights go up, lower right, as in Act One in the transi-
tion from the Court room to the Stevens living room,
though instead of the living room, the scene is now
Temple's private apartment. A door, left, enters from
the house proper. A door, right, leads into the nursery
where the child is asleep in its crib. At rear, french windows open onto a terrace; this is a private entrance to
the house itself from outdoors. At left, a closet door
stands open. Garments are scattered over the floor about
it, indicating that the closet has been searched, not hurriedly so much as savagely and ruthlessly and thoroughly. At right, is a fireplace of gas logs. A desk against
the rear wall is open and shows traces of the same savage
and ruthless search. A table, center, bears Temple's hat,
gloves and bag, also a bag such as is associated with
infants; two bags, obviously Temple's, are packed and
closed and sit on the floor beside the table. The whole
room indicates Temple's imminent departure, and that
something has been vainly yet savagely and completely,
perhaps even frantically, searched for.

When the lights go up, Pete is standing in the open
closet door, holding a final garment, a negligee, in his
hands. He is about 25. He does not look like a criminal.
That is, he is not a standardised recognisable criminal or

gangster type, quite. He looks almost like the general conception of a college man, or a successful young automobile or appliance salesman. His clothes are ordinary, neither flashy nor sharp, simply what everybody wears. But there is a definite 'untamed' air to him. He is handsome, attractive to women, not at all unpredictable because you—or they—know exactly what he will do, you just hope he wont do it this time. He has a hard, ruthless quality, not immoral but unmoral.

He wears a light-weight summer suit, his hat is shoved onto the back of his head so that, engaged as he is at present, he looks exactly like a youthful city detective in a tough moving picture. He is searching the flimsy negligee, quickly and without gentleness, drops it and turns, finds his feet entangled in the other garments on the floor and without pausing, kicks himself free and crosses to the desk and stands looking down at the litter on it which he has already searched thoroughly and savagely once, with a sort of bleak and contemptuous disgust.

Temple enters, left. She wears a dark suit for traveling beneath a lightweight open coat, is hatless, carries the fur coat which we have seen, and a child's robe or blanket over the same arm, and a filled milk bottle in the other hand. She pauses long enough to glance at the littered room. Then she comes on in and approaches the table. Pete turns his head; except for that, he doesn't move.

PETE

Well?

TEMPLE

No. The people where she lives say they haven't seen her since she left to come to work this morning.

PETE

I could have told you that.
> (he glances at his wrist watch)

We've still got time. Where does she live?

TEMPLE
> (at the table)

And then what? hold a lighted cigarette against the sole of her foot?

PETE

It's fifty dollars, even if you are accustomed yourself to thinking in hundreds. Besides the jewelry. What do you suggest then? call the cops?

TEMPLE

No. You wont have to run. I'm giving you an out.

PETE

An out?

TEMPLE

No dough, no snatch. Isn't that how you would say it?

PETE

Maybe I dont get you.

TEMPLE

You can quit now. Clear out. Leave. Get out from under. Save yourself. Then all you'll have to do is, wait till my husband gets back, and start over.

PETE

Maybe I still dont get you.

TEMPLE

You've still got the letters, haven't you?

PETE

Oh, the letters.

He reaches inside his coat, takes out the packet of letters and tosses it onto the table.

There you are.

TEMPLE

I told you two days ago I didn't want them.

PETE

Sure. That was two days ago.

They watch each other a moment. Then Temple dumps the fur coat and the robe from her arm, onto the table, sets the bottle carefully on the table, takes up the packet of letters and extends her other hand to Pete.

TEMPLE

Give me your lighter.

Pete produces the lighter from his pocket and hands it to her. That is, he extends it, not moving otherwise, so that she has to take a step or two toward him to reach and take it. Then she turns and crosses to the hearth, snaps the lighter on. It misses fire two or three times, then lights. Pete has not moved, watching her. She stands motionless a moment, the packet of letters in one hand, the burning lighter in the other. Then she turns her head and looks back at him. For another moment they watch each other.

PETE

Go ahead. Burn them. The other time I gave them to you, you turned them down so you could always change your mind and back out. Burn them.

They watch each other for another moment. Then she turns her head and stands now, her face averted, the lighter still burning. Pete watches her for another moment.

Then put that junk down and come here.

She snaps out the lighter, turns, crosses to the table, putting the packet of letters and the lighter on the table as she passes it, and goes on to where Pete has not moved. At this moment, Nancy appears in the door, left. Neither of them sees her. Pete puts his arms around Temple.

I offered you an out too.
> (he draws her closer)

Baby.

TEMPLE

Dont call me that.

PETE

> (tightens his arms, caressing and savage too)

Red did. I'm as good a man as he was. Aint I?

They kiss. Nancy moves quietly through the door and stops just inside the room, watching them. She now wears the standardised department-store maidservant's uniform, but without cap and apron, beneath a lightweight open topcoat; on her head is a battered almost shapeless felt hat which must have once belonged to a man. Pete breaks the kiss.

Come on. Let's get out of here. I've even got
moral or something. I dont even want to put my
hands on you in his house—

He sees Nancy across Temple's shoulder, and reacts.
Temple reacts to him, turns quickly and sees Nancy too.
Nancy comes on into the room.

> **TEMPLE**
> (to Nancy)

What are you doing here?

> **NANCY**

I brought my foot. So he can hold that cigarette
against it.

> **TEMPLE**

So you're not just a thief: you're a spy too.

> **PETE**

Maybe she's not a thief either. Maybe she brought
it back.
> (they watch Nancy, who
> doesn't answer)

Or maybe she didn't. Maybe we had better use
that cigarette.
> (to Nancy)

How about it? Is that what you came back for, sure enough?

TEMPLE
(to Pete)
Hush. Take the bags and go on to the car.

PETE
(to Temple but watching Nancy)
I'll wait for you. There may be a little something I can do here, after all.

TEMPLE
Go on, I tell you! Let's for God's sake get away from here. Go on.

Pete watches Nancy for a moment longer, who stands facing them but not looking at anything, motionless, almost bemused, her face sad, brooding and inscrutable. Then Pete turns, goes to the table, picks up the lighter, seems about to pass on, then pauses again and with almost infinitesimal hesitation takes up the packet of letters, puts it back inside his coat, takes up the two packed bags and crosses to the french window, passing Nancy, who is still looking at nothing and no one.

PETE
(to Nancy)
Not that I wouldn't like to, you know. For less than fifty bucks even. For old lang syne.

He transfers the bags to one hand, opens the french window, starts to exit, pauses half way out and looks back at Temple.

> I'll be listening, in case you change your mind about the cigarette.

He goes on out, draws the door to after him. Just before it closes, Nancy speaks.

NANCY

Wait.

Pete stops, begins to open the door again.

TEMPLE
(quickly: to Pete)
Go on! Go on! For God's sake go on!

Pete exits, shuts the door after him. Nancy and Temple face each other.

NANCY

Maybe I was wrong to think that just hiding that money and diamonds was going to stop you. Maybe I ought to have give it to him yesterday as soon as I found where you had hid it. Then wouldn't nobody between here and Chicago or Texas seen anything of him but his dust.

TEMPLE

So you did steal it. And you saw what good that
did, didn't you?

NANCY

If you can call it stealing, then so can I. Because wasn't but part of it yours to begin with.
Just the diamonds was yours. Not to mention
that money is almost two thousand dollars, that
you told me was just two hundred and that you
told him was even less than that, just fifty. No
wonder he wasn't worried—about just fifty dollars. He wouldn't even be worried if he knowed
it was even the almost two thousand it is, let
alone the two hundred you told me it was. He
aint even worried about whether or not you'll
have any money at all when you get out to the
car. He knows that all he's got to do is, just wait
and keep his hand on you and maybe just mash
hard enough with it, and you'll get another pas-
sel of money and diamonds too out of your husband or your pa. Only, this time he'll have his
hand on you and you'll have a little trouble telling him it's just fifty dollars instead of almost two
thousand—

Temple steps quickly forward and slaps Nancy across
the face. Nancy steps back. As she does so, the packet
of money and the jewel box fall to the floor from inside

her topcoat. Temple stops, looking down at the money and jewels. Nancy recovers.

Yes, there it is, that caused all the grief and ruin. If you hadn't been somebody that would have a box of diamonds and a husband that you could find almost two thousand dollars in his britches pocket while he was asleep, that man wouldn't have tried to sell you them letters. Maybe if I hadn't taken and hid it, you would have give it to him before you come to this. Or maybe if I had just give it to him yesterday and got the letters, or maybe if I was to take it out to where he's waiting in that car right now, and say, Here, man, take your money—

TEMPLE

Try it. Pick it up and take it out to him, and see. If you'll wait until I finish packing, you can even carry the bag.

NANCY

I know. It aint even the letters any more. Maybe it never was. It was already there in whoever could write the kind of letters that even eight years afterward could still make grief and ruin. The letters never did matter. You could have got them back at any time; he even tried to give them to you twice—

TEMPLE

How much spying have you been doing?

NANCY

All of it.—You wouldn't even needed money
and diamonds to get them back. A woman dont
need it. All she needs is womanishness to get
anything she wants from men. You could have
done that right here in the house, without even
tricking your husband into going off fishing.

TEMPLE

A perfect example of whore morality. But then,
if I can say whore, so can you, cant you? Maybe
the difference is, I decline to be one in my husband's house.

NANCY

I aint talking about your husband. I aint even
talking about you. I'm talking about two little
children.

TEMPLE

So am I. Why else do you think I sent Bucky on
to his grandmother, except to get him out of a
house where the man he has been taught to call
his father, may at any moment decide to tell
him he has none? As clever a spy as you must
surely have heard my husband—

NANCY

(interrupts)

I've heard him. And I heard you too. You fought back—that time. Not for yourself, but for that little child. But now you have quit.

TEMPLE

Quit?

NANCY

Yes. You gave up. You gave up the child too. Willing to risk never seeing him again maybe.

(Temple doesn't answer)

That's right. You dont need to make no excuses to me. Just tell me what you must have already strengthened your mind up to telling all the rest of the folks that are going to ask you that. You are willing to risk it. Is that right?

(Temple doesn't answer)

All right. We'll say you have answered it. So that settles Bucky. Now answer me this one. Who are you going to leave the other one with?

TEMPLE

Leave her with? A six-months-old baby?

NANCY

That's right. Of course you cant leave her. Not with nobody. You cant no more leave a six-

months-old baby with nobody while you run
away from your husband with another man, than
you can take a six-months-old baby with you on
that trip. That's what I'm talking about. So maybe
you'll just leave it in there in that cradle; it'll
cry for a while, but it's too little to cry very
loud and so maybe wont nobody hear it and
come meddling, especially with the house shut
up and locked until Mr Gowan gets back next
week, and probably by that time it will have
hushed—

TEMPLE
Are you really trying to make me hit you again?

NANCY
Or maybe taking her with you will be just as
easy, at least until the first time you write Mr
Gowan or your pa for money and they dont send
it as quick as your new man thinks they ought
to, and he throws you and the baby both out.
Then you can just drop it into a garbage can
and no more trouble to you or anybody, because
then you will be rid of both of them—

> (Temple makes a convul-
> sive movement, then catches
> herself)

Hit me. Light you a cigarette too. I told you and
him both I brought my foot. Here it is.

> (she raises her foot slightly)

I've tried everything else; I reckon I can try that
too.

TEMPLE
(repressed, furious)
Hush. I tell you for the last time. Hush.

NANCY
I've hushed.

She doesn't move. She is not looking at Temple. There
is a slight change in her voice or manner, though we
only realise later that she is not addressing Temple.

I've tried. I've tried everything I know. You can
see that.

TEMPLE
Which nobody will dispute. You threatened me
with my children, and even with my husband—
if you can call my husband a threat. You even
stole my elopement money. Oh yes, nobody will
dispute that you tried. Though at least you
brought the money back. Pick it up.

NANCY
You said you dont need it.

TEMPLE
I dont. Pick it up.

NANCY

No more do I need it.

TEMPLE

Pick it up, anyway. You can keep your next week's pay out of it when you give it back to Mr Gowan.

Nancy stoops and gathers up the money, and gathers the jewelry back into its box, and puts them on the table.

(quieter)

Nancy.

(Nancy looks at her)

I'm sorry. Why do you force me to this—hitting and screaming at you, when you have always been so good to my children and me—my husband too—all of us—trying to hold us together in a household, a family, that anybody should have known all the time couldn't possibly hold together? even in decency, let alone happiness?

NANCY

I reckon I'm ignorant. I dont know that yet. Besides, I aint talking about any household or happiness neither—

TEMPLE

(with sharp command)

Nancy!

NANCY

—I'm talking about two little children—

TEMPLE

I said, hush.

NANCY

I cant hush. I'm going to ask you one more time.
Are you going to do it?

TEMPLE

Yes!

NANCY

Maybe I am ignorant. You got to say it out in
words yourself, so I can hear them. Say, I'm
going to do it.

TEMPLE

You heard me. I'm going to do it.

NANCY

Money or no money.

TEMPLE

Money or no money.

NANCY

Children or no children.
                    (Temple doesn't answer)
To leave one with a man that's willing to believe

the child aint got no father, willing to take the other one to a man that dont even want no children—

(They stare at one another)

If you can do it, you can say it.

TEMPLE

Yes! Children or no children! Now get out of here. Take your part of that money, and get out. Here—

Temple goes quickly to the table, removes two or three bills from the mass of banknotes, and hands them to Nancy, who takes them. Temple takes up the rest of the money, takes up her bag from the table and opens it. Nancy crosses quietly toward the nursery, picking up the milk bottle from the table as she passes, and goes on. With the open bag in one hand and the money in the other, Temple notices Nancy's movement.

What are you doing?

NANCY

(still moving)

This bottle has got cold. I'm going to warm it in the bathroom.

Then Nancy stops and looks back at Temple, with something so strange in her look that Temple, about to resume putting the money into the bag, pauses too, watching Nancy. When Nancy speaks, it is like the former speech: we dont realise until afterward what it signifies.

I tried everything I knowed. You can see that.

TEMPLE
(peremptory, commanding)
Nancy.

NANCY
(quietly, turning on)
I've hushed.

She exits through the door into the nursery. Temple finishes putting the money into the bag, and closes it and puts it back on the table. Then she turns to the baby's bag. She tidies it, checks rapidly over its contents, takes up the jewel box and stows it in the bag and closes the bag. All this takes about two minutes; she has just closed the bag when Nancy emerges quietly from the nursery, without the milk bottle, and crosses, pausing at the table only long enough to put back on it the money Temple gave her, then starts on toward the opposite door through which she first entered the room.

TEMPLE

Now what?

Nancy goes on toward the other door. Temple watches
her.

Nancy.

> (Nancy pauses, still not
> looking back)

Dont think too hard of me.

> (Nancy waits, immobile,
> looking at nothing. When
> Temple doesn't continue, she
> moves again toward the
> door)

If I—it ever comes up, I'll tell everybody you
did your best. You tried. But you were right.
It wasn't even the letters. It was me.

> (Nancy moves on)

Good-bye, Nancy.

> (Nancy reaches the door)

You've got your key. I'll leave your money here
on the table. You can get it—

> (Nancy exits)

Nancy!

There is no answer. Temple looks a moment longer at
the empty door, shrugs, moves, takes up the money
Nancy left, glances about, crosses to the littered desk
and takes up a paperweight and returns to the table and
puts the money beneath the weight; now moving rapidly

and with determination, she takes up the blanket from
the table and crosses to the nursery door and exits
through it. A second or two, then she screams. The lights
flicker and begin to dim, fade swiftly into complete
darkness, over the scream.

The stage is in complete darkness.

Same as Scene I. Governor's Office. 3:09 A.M. March
twelfth.

The lights go on upper left. The scene is the same as
before, Scene I, except that Gowan Stevens now sits
in the chair behind the desk where the Governor had been
sitting and the Governor is no longer in the room. Temple
now kneels before the desk, facing it, her arms on the
desk and her face buried in her arms. Stevens now stands
beside and over her. The hands of the clock show nine
minutes past three.

Temple does not know that the Governor has gone
and that her husband is now in the room

> TEMPLE
>> (her face still hidden)
> And that's all. The police came, and the mur-
> deress still sitting in a chair in the kitchen in
> the dark, saying 'Yes, Lord, I done it,' and
> then in the cell at the jail still saying it—
>>> (Stevens leans and touches
>>> her arm, as if to help her up.
>>> She resists, though still not
>>> raising her head)
> Not yet. It's my cue to stay down here until
> his honor or excellency grants our plea, isn't it?

Or have I already missed my cue forever even if the sovereign state should offer me a hand-kerchief right out of its own elected public suffrage dressing-gown pocket? Because see?

>   (she raises her face, quite
>   blindly, tearless, still not
>   looking toward the chair
>   where she could see Gowan
>   instead of the Governor, in-
>   to the full glare of the light)

Still no tears.

STEVENS

Get up, Temple.

>   (he starts to lift her again,
>   but before he can do so, she
>   rises herself, standing, her
>   face still turned away from
>   the desk, still blind; she puts
>   her arm up almost in the
>   gesture of a little girl about
>   to cry, but instead she merely
>   shields her eyes from the
>   light while her pupils read-
>   just)

TEMPLE

Nor cigarette either; this time it certainly won't take long, since all he has to say is, No.

(still not turning her face to
look, even though she is now
speaking directly to the Governor whom she still thinks
is sitting behind the desk)

Because you aren't going to save her, are you?
Because all this was not for the sake of her
soul because her soul doesn't need it, but for
mine.

STEVENS

(gently)

Why not finish first? Tell the rest of it. You had
started to say something about the jail.

TEMPLE

The jail. They had the funeral the next day—
Gowan had barely reached New Orleans, so he
chartered an airplane back that morning—and
in Jefferson, everything going to the graveyard
passes the jail, or going anywhere else for that
matter, passing right under the upstairs barred
windows—the bullpen and the cells where the
Negro prisoners—the crapshooters and whiskey-
peddlers and vagrants and the murderers and
murderesses too—can look down and enjoy it,
enjoy the funerals too. Like this. Some white
person you know is in a jail or a hospital, and
right off you say, How ghastly: not at the shame

or the pain, but the walls, the locks, and before you even know it, you have sent them books to read, cards, puzzles to play with. But not Negroes. You dont even think about the cards and puzzles and books. And so all of a sudden you find out with a kind of terror, that they have not only escaped having to read, they have escaped having to escape. So whenever you pass the jail, you can see them—no, not them, you dont see them at all, you just see the hands among the bars of the windows, not tapping or fidgeting or even holding, gripping the bars like white hands would be, but just lying there among the interstices, not just at rest, but even restful, already shaped and easy and unanguished to the handles of the plows and axes and hoes, and the mops and brooms and the rockers of white folks' cradles, until even the steel bars fitted them too without alarm or anguish. You see? not gnarled and twisted with work at all, but even limbered and suppled by it, smoothed and even softened, as though with only the penny-change of simple sweat they had already got the same thing the white ones have to pay dollars by the ounce jar for. Not immune to work, and in compromise with work is not the right word either, but in confederacy with work and so free from it; in armistice, peace;—the same long supple hands serene and immune to anguish, so that all the

owners of them need to look out with, to see with
—to look out at the outdoors—the funerals, the
passing, the people, the freedom, the sunlight,
the free air—are just the hands: not the eyes:
just the hands lying there among the bars and
looking out, that can see the shape of the plow
or hoe or axe before daylight comes; and even
in the dark, without even having to turn on the
light, can not only find the child, the baby—not
her child but yours, the white one—but the
trouble and discomfort too—the hunger, the wet
didy, the unfastened safety-pin—and see to rem-
edy it. You see. If I could just cry. There was
another one, a man this time, before my time in
Jefferson but Uncle Gavin will remember this
too. His wife had just died—they had been married only two weeks—and he buried her and so
at first he tried just walking the country roads at
night for exhaustion and sleep, only that failed
and then he tried getting drunk so he could sleep,
and that failed and then he tried fighting and
then he cut a white man's throat with a razor in
a dice game and so at last he could sleep for a
little while; which was where the sheriff found
him, asleep on the wooden floor of the gallery
of the house he had rented for his wife, his marriage, his life, his old age. Only that waked him
up, and so in the jail that afternoon, all of a
sudden it took the jailer and a deputy and five

other Negro prisoners just to throw him down and hold him while they locked the chains on him—lying there on the floor with more than a half dozen men panting to hold him down, and what do you think he said? 'Look like I just cant quit thinking. Look like I just cant quit.'

> (she ceases, blinking, rubs her eyes and then extends one hand blindly toward Stevens, who has already shaken out his handkerchief and hands it to her. There are still no tears on her face; she merely takes the handkerchief and dabs, pats at her eyes with it as if it were a powderpuff, talking again)

But we have passed the jail, haven't we? We're in the courtroom now. It was the same there; Uncle Gavin had rehearsed her, of course, which was easy, since all you can say when they ask you to answer to a murder charge is, Not Guilty. Otherwise, they cant even have a trial; they would have to hurry out and find another murderer before they could take the next official step. So they asked her, all correct and formal among the judges and lawyers and bailiffs and jury and the Scales and the Sword and the flag and the ghosts of Coke upon Littleton upon Bonaparte and Julius Caesar and all the rest of it, not to mention the eyes and the faces which were getting a moving-picture show for free since they had already paid for it in the taxes, and nobody really listening since there was only one thing she could say. Except that she didn't say it: just raising her head enough to be heard plain—not loud: just plain—and said, 'Guilty, Lord'—like that, disrupting and confounding and dispersing and flinging back two thousand years, the whole edifice of corpus juris and rules of evidence we have been working to make stand up by itself ever since Caesar, like when without even watching yourself or even knowing you were doing it, you would reach out your hand and turn over a chip and expose to air and light and vision the frantic and aghast turmoil of an antbed. And moved the chip again, when even the ants must have thought there couldn't be another one within her reach: when they finally explained to her that to say she was not guilty, had nothing to do with truth but only with law, and this time she said it right, Not Guilty, and so then the jury could tell her she lied and everything was all correct again and, as everybody thought, even safe, since now she wouldn't be asked to say anything at all any more. Only, they were wrong; the jury said Guilty and the judge said Hang and now everybody was already pick-

ing up his hat to go home, when she picked up
that chip too: the judge said, 'And may God
have mercy on your soul' and Nancy answered:
'Yes, Lord.'

> (she turns suddenly, almost
> briskly, speaking so briskly
> that her momentum carries
> her on past the instant when
> she sees and recognizes
> Gowan sitting where she had
> thought all the time that the
> Governor was sitting and
> listening to her)

And that is all, this time. And so now you can tell
us. I know you're not going to save her, but
now you can say so. It won't be difficult. Just
one word—

> (she stops, arrested, utterly
> motionless, but even then she
> is first to recover)

Oh God.

> (G o w a n rises quickly.
> Temple whirls to Stevens)

Why is it you must always believe in plants?
Do you have to? Is it because you have to? Because you are a lawyer? No, I'm wrong. I'm
sorry; I was the one that started us hiding
gimmicks on each other, wasn't it?

> (quickly: turning to Gowan)

Of course; you didn't take the sleeping pill at all. Which means you didn't even need to come here for the Governor to hide you behind the door or under the desk or wherever it was he was trying to tell me you were hiding and listening, because after all the Governor of a Southern state has got to try to act like he regrets having to aberrate from being a gentleman—

STEVENS
(to Temple)
Stop it.

GOWAN
Maybe we both didn't start hiding soon enough —by about eight years—not in desk drawers either, but in two abandoned mine shafts, one in Siberia and the other at the South Pole, maybe.

TEMPLE
All right. I didn't mean hiding. I'm sorry.

GOWAN
Dont be. Just draw on your eight years' interest for that.
(to Stevens)
All right, all right; tell me to shut up too.
(to no one directly)
In fact, this may be the time for me to start saying sorry for the next eight-year term. Just give me a little time. Eight years of gratitude might

be a habit a little hard to break. So here goes.

(to Temple)

I'm sorry. Forget it.

TEMPLE

I would have told you.

GOWAN

You did. Forget it. You see how easy it is? You could have been doing that yourself for eight years: every time I would say 'Say sorry, please,' all you would need would be to answer: 'I did. Forget it.'

(to Stevens)

I guess that's all, isn't it? We can go home now.

(he starts to come around the desk)

TEMPLE

Wait.

(Gowan stops; they look at each other)

Where are you going?

GOWAN

I said home, didn't I? To pick up Bucky and carry him back to his own bed again.

(they look at one another)

You're not even going to ask me where he is now?

(answers himself)

Where we always leave our children when the clutch—

STEVENS

(to Gowan)

Maybe I will say shut up this time.

GOWAN

Only let me finish first. I was going to say, 'with our handiest kinfolks.'

(to Temple)

I carried him to Maggie's.

STEVENS

(moving)

I think we can all go now. Come on.

GOWAN

So do I.

(he comes on around the desk, and stops again; to Temple)

Make up your mind. Do you want to ride with me, or Gavin?

STEVENS

(to Gowan)

Go on. You can pick up Bucky.

GOWAN

Right.

> (he turns, starts toward the
> steps front, where Temple
> and Stevens entered, then
> stops)

That's right. I'm probably still supposed to use the spy's entrance.

> (he turns back, starts
> around the desk again,
> toward the door at rear,
> sees Temple's gloves and bag
> on the desk, and takes them
> up and holds them out to
> her: roughly almost)

Here. This is what they call evidence; dont forget these.

> (Temple takes the bag and
> gloves. Gowan goes on
> toward the door at rear)

TEMPLE

> (after him)

Did you have a hat and coat?

> (he doesn't answer. He goes
> on, exits)

Oh God. Again.

STEVENS
(touches her arm)

Come on.

TEMPLE
(not moving yet)

Tomorrow and tomorrow and tomorrow—

STEVENS
(speaking her thought, finishing the sentence)

—he will wreck the car again against the wrong
tree, in the wrong place, and you will have to
forgive him again, for the next eight years until
he can wreck the car again in the wrong place,
against the wrong tree—

TEMPLE

I was driving it too. I was driving some of the
time too.

STEVENS
(gently)

Then let that comfort you.
(he takes her arm again,
turns her toward the stairs)

Come on. It's late.

TEMPLE
(holds back)

Wait. He said, No.

STEVENS

Yes.

TEMPLE

Did he say why?

STEVENS

Yes. He cant.

TEMPLE

Cant? The Governor of a state, with all the legal
power to pardon or at least reprieve, cant?

STEVENS

That's just law. If it was only law, I could have
plead insanity for her at any time, without bringing you here at two oclock in the morning—

TEMPLE

And the other parent too; dont forget that. I
dont know yet how you did it. . . . Yes, Gowan
was here first; he was just pretending to be
asleep when I carried Bucky in and put him in
his bed; yes, that was what you called that leak-
ing valve, when we stopped at the filling station
to change the wheel: to let him get ahead of us—

STEVENS

All right. He wasn't even talking about justice.
He was talking about a child, a little boy—

TEMPLE

That's right. Make it good: the same little boy
to hold whose normal and natural home together,
the murderess, the nigger, the dopefiend whore,
didn't hesitate to cast the last gambit—and
maybe that's the wrong word too, isn't it?—she
knew and had: her own debased and worthless
life. Oh yes, I know that answer too; that was
brought out here tonight too: that a little child
shall not suffer in order to come unto Me. So
good can come out of evil.

STEVENS

It not only can, it must.

TEMPLE

So *touché*, then. Because what kind of natural
and normal home can that little boy have where
his father may at any time tell him he has no
father?

STEVENS

Haven't you been answering that question every
day for six years? Didn't Nancy answer it for
you when she told you how you had fought back,
not for yourself, but for that little boy? Not to
show the father that he was wrong, nor even to
prove to the little boy that the father was wrong,
but to let the little boy learn with his own eyes

that nothing, not even that, which could possibly enter that house, could ever harm him?

TEMPLE
But I quit. Nancy told you that too.

STEVENS
She doesn't think so now. Isn't that what she's going to prove Friday morning?

TEMPLE
Friday. The black day. The day you never start on a journey. Except that Nancy's journey didn't start at daylight or sunup or whenever it is polite and tactful to hang people, day after tomorrow. Her journey started that morning eight years ago when I got on the train at the University—

> (she stops: a moment; then
> quietly)

Oh God, that was Friday too; that baseball game was Friday—

> (rapidly)

You see? Dont you see? It's nowhere near enough yet. Of course he wouldn't save her. If he did that, it would be over: Gowan could just throw me out, which he may do yet, or I could throw Gowan out, which I could have done until it got too late now, too late forever now, or the judge could have thrown us both out and given Bucky to an orphanage, and it would be all over. But now it can go on, tomorrow and tomorrow and tomorrow, forever and forever and forever—

STEVENS
(gently tries to start her)
Come on.

TEMPLE
(holding back)
Tell me exactly what he did say. Not tonight: it couldn't have been tonight—or did he say it over the telephone, and we didn't even need—

STEVENS
He said it a week ago—

TEMPLE
Yes, about the same time when you sent the wire. What did he say?

STEVENS
(quotes)
'Who am I, to have the brazen temerity and hardihood to set the puny appanage of my office in the balance against that simple undeviable aim? Who am I, to render null and abrogate the purchase she made with that poor crazed lost and worthless life?'

TEMPLE
(wildly)
And good too—good and mellow too. So it was not even in hopes of saving her life, that I came here at two o'clock in the morning. It wasn't even to be told that he had already decided not to save her. It was not even to confess to my husband, but to do it in the hearing of two strangers, something which I had spent eight years trying to expiate so that my husband wouldn't have to know about it. Dont you see? That's just suffering. Not for anything: just suffering.

STEVENS
You came here to affirm the very thing which Nancy is going to die tomorrow morning to postulate: that little children, as long as they are little children, shall be intact, unanguished, untorn, unterrified.

TEMPLE
(quietly)
All right. I have done that. Can we go home now?

STEVENS
Yes.
(she turns, moves toward
the steps, Stevens beside her.
As she reaches the first step,

(she falters, seems to stumble
slightly, like a sleepwalker.
Stevens steadies her, but at
once she frees her arm, and
begins to descend)

TEMPLE
(on the first step: to no one,
still with that sleepwalker
air)
To save my soul—if I have a soul. If there is a
God to save it—a God who wants it—

(Curtain)

ACT THREE

THE JAIL (Nor Even Yet Quite Relinquish———)

So, although in a sense the jail was both older and less old than the courthouse, in actuality, in time, in observation and memory, it was older even than the town itself. Because there was no town until there was a courthouse, and no courthouse until (like some unsentient unweaned creature torn violently from the dug of its dam) the floorless lean-to rabbit-hutch housing the iron chest was reft from the log flank of the jail and transmogrified into a by-neo-Greek-out-of-Georgian-England edifice set in the center of what in time would be the town Square (as a result of which, the town itself had moved one block south—or rather, no town then and yet, the courthouse itself the catalyst: a mere dusty widening of the trace, trail, pathway in a forest of oak and ash and hickory and sycamore and flowering catalpa and dogwood and judas tree and persimmon and wild plum, with on one side old Alec Holston's tavern and coaching-yard, and a little farther along, Ratcliffe's trading-post-store and the blacksmith's, and diagonal to all of them, *en face* and solitary beyond the dust, the log jail; moved—the town—complete and intact, one block southward, so that now, a century and a quarter later, the coaching-yard and Ratcliffe's store were gone and old Alec's tavern and the blacksmith's were a hotel and a garage, on a main thoroughfare true enough but still a business side-street, and the jail across from them, though transformed also now into two storeys of Georgian brick by the hand ((or anyway pocketbooks)) of Sartoris and Sutpen and Louis Grenier, faced not even on a side-street but on an alley);

And so, being older than all, it had seen all: the mutation and the change: and, in that sense, had recorded them (indeed, as Gavin Stevens, the town lawyer and the county amateur Cincinnatus, was wont to say, if you would peruse in unbroken—ay, overlapping—continuity the history of a community, look not in the church registers and the courthouse records, but beneath the successive layers of calcimine and creosote and whitewash on the walls of the jail, since only in that forcible carceration does man find the idleness in which to compose, in the gross and simple terms of his gross and simple lusts and yearnings, the gross and simple recapitulations of his gross and simple heart); invisible and impacted, not only beneath the annual inside creosote-and-whitewash of bullpen and cell, but on the blind outside walls too, first the simple mud-chinked log ones and then the symmetric brick, not only the scrawled illiterate repetitive unimaginative doggerel and the perspectiveless almost prehistoric sexual picture-writing, but the images, the panorama not only of the town but of its days and years until a century and better had been accomplished, filled not only with its mutation and change from a halting-place: to a community: to a settlement: to a village: to a town, but with the shapes and motions, the gestures of passion and hope and travail and endurance, of the men

and women and children in their successive overlapping
generations long after the subjects which had reflected
the images were vanished and replaced and again replaced, as when you stand say alone in a dim and empty
room and believe, hypnotised beneath the vast weight of
man's incredible and enduring *Was*, that perhaps by
turning your head aside you will see from the corner of
your eye the turn of a moving limb—a gleam of crin-
oline, a laced wrist, perhaps even a Cavalier plume—
who knows? provided there is will enough, perhaps even
the face itself three hundred years after it was dust—
the eyes, two jellied tears filled with arrogance and
pride and satiety and knowledge of anguish and fore-
knowledge of death, saying no to death across twelve
generations, asking still the old same unanswerable question three centuries after that which reflected them had
learned that the answer didn't matter, or—better still—
had forgotten the asking of it—in the shadowy fathom-
less dreamlike depths of an old mirror which has looked
at too much too long;

But not in shadow, not this one, this mirror, these logs:
squatting in the full glare of the stump-pocked clearing
during those first summers, solitary on its side of the
dusty widening marked with an occasional wheel but
mostly by the prints of horses and men: Pettigrew's private pony express until he and it were replaced by a
monthly stagecoach from Memphis, the race horse which
Jason Compson traded to Ikkemotubbe, old Mohataha's
son and the last ruling Chickasaw chief in that section,

for a square of land so large that, as the first formal sur-
vey revealed, the new courthouse would have been only
another of Compson's outbuildings had not the town
Corporation bought enough of it (at Compson's price)
to forefend themselves being trespassers, and the saddle-
mare which bore Doctor Habersham's worn black bag
(and which drew the buggy after Doctor Habersham got
too old and stiff to mount the saddle), and the mules
which drew the wagon in which, seated in a rocking chair
beneath a French parasol held by a Negro slave girl, old
Mohataha would come to town on Saturdays (and came
that last time to set her capital X on the paper which
ratified the dispossession of her people forever, coming
in the wagon that time too, barefoot as always but in the
purple silk dress which her son, Ikkemotubbe, had
brought her back from France, and a hat crowned with
the royal-colored plume of a queen, beneath the slave-
held parasol still and with another female slave child
squatting on her other side holding the crusted slippers
which she had never been able to get her feet into, and
in the back of the wagon the petty rest of the unmarked
Empire flotsam her son had brought to her which was
small enough to be moved; driving for the last time out
of the woods into the dusty widening before Ratcliffe's
store where the Federal land agent and his marshal
waited for her with the paper, and stopped the mules
and sat for a little time, the young men of her bodyguard
squatting quietly about the halted wagon after the eight-
mile walk, while from the gallery of the store and of
Holston's tavern the settlement—the Ratcliffes and

Compsons and Peabodys and Pettigrews ((not Grenier
and Holston and Habersham, because Louis Grenier declined to come in to see it, and for the same reason old
Alec Holston sat alone on that hot afternoon before the
smoldering log in the fireplace of his taproom, and Doctor Habersham was dead and his son had already departed for the West with his bride, who was Mohataha's
granddaughter, and his father-in-law, Mohataha's son,
Ikkemotubbe))—looked on, watched: the inscrutable
ageless wrinkled face, the fat shapeless body dressed in
the cast-off garments of a French queen, which on her
looked like the Sunday costume of the madam of a rich
Natchez or New Orleans brothel, sitting in a battered
wagon inside a squatting ring of her household troops,
her young men dressed in their Sunday clothes for traveling too: then she said, 'Where is this Indian territory?'
And they told her: West. 'Turn the mules west,' she said,
and someone did so, and she took the pen from the
agent and made her X on the paper and handed the pen
back and the wagon moved, the young men rising too, and
she vanished so across that summer afternoon to that
terrific and infinitesimal creak and creep of ungreased
wheels, herself immobile beneath the rigid parasol,
grotesque and regal, bizarre and moribund, like obsolescence's self riding off the stage enthroned on its own
obsolete catafalque, looking not once back, not once back
toward home);

But most of all, the prints of men—the fitted shoes
which Doctor Habersham and Louis Grenier had brought

from the Atlantic seaboard, the cavalry boots in which Alec Holston had ridden behind Francis Marion, and—more myriad almost than leaves, outnumbering all the others lumped together—the moccasins, the deerhide sandals of the forest, worn not by the Indians but by white men, the pioneers, the long hunters, as though they had not only vanquished the wilderness but had even stepped into the very footgear of them they dispossessed (and mete and fitting so, since it was by means of his feet and legs that the white man conquered America; the closed and split U's of his horses and cattle overlay his own prints always, merely consolidating his victory);—(the jail) watched them all, red men and white and black—the pioneers, the hunters, the forest men with rifles, who made the same light rapid soundless toed-in almost heelless prints as the red men they dispossessed and who in fact dispossessed the red men for that reason: not because of the grooved barrel but because they could enter the red man's milieu and make the same footprints that he made; the husbandman printing deep the hard heels of his brogans because of the weight he bore on his shoulders: axe and saw and plow-stock, who dispossessed the forest man for the obverse reason: because with his saw and axe he simply removed, obliterated, the milieu in which alone the forest man could exist; then the land speculators and the traders in slaves and whiskey who followed the husbandmen, and the politicians who followed the land speculators, printing deeper and deeper the dust of that dusty widening, until at last there was no mark of Chickasaw left in it any more; watching (the jail) them all, from the first innocent days when Doctor Habersham and his son and Alex Holston and Louis Grenier were first guests and then friends of Ikkemotubbe's Chickasaw clan; then an Indian agent and a land-office and a trading-post, and suddenly Ikkemotubbe and his Chickasaws were themselves the guests without being friends of the Federal Government; then Ratcliffe, and the trading-post was no longer simply an Indian trading-post, though Indians were still welcome, of course (since, after all, they owned the land or anyway were on it first and claimed it), then Compson with his race horse and presently Compson began to own the Indian accounts for tobacco and calico and jeans pants and cooking-pots on Ratcliffe's books (in time he would own Ratcliffe's books too) and one day Ikkemotubbe owned the race horse and Compson owned the land itself, some of which the city fathers would have to buy from him at his price in order to establish a town; and Pettigrew with his tri-weekly mail, and then a monthly stage and the new faces coming in faster than old Alex Holston, arthritic and irascible, hunkered like an old surly bear over his smoldering hearth even in the heat of summer (he alone now of that original three, since old Grenier no longer came in to the settlement, and old Doctor Habersham was dead, and the old doctor's son, in the opinion of the settlement, had already turned Indian and renegade even at the age of twelve or fourteen) any longer made any effort, wanted, to associate

names with; and now indeed the last moccasin print
vanished from that dusty widening, the last toed-in
heelless light soft quick long-striding print pointing west
for an instant, then trodden from the sight and memory
of man by a heavy leather heel engaged not in the traffic
of endurance and hardihood and survival, but in money
—taking with it (the print) not only the moccasins but
the deer-hide leggins and jerkin too, because Ikkemotubbe's Chickasaws now wore Eastern factory-made
jeans and shoes sold them on credit out of Ratcliffe's and
Compson's general store, walking in to the settlement
on the white man's Saturday, carrying the alien shoes
rolled neatly in the alien pants under their arms, to
stop at the bridge over Compson's creek long enough
to bathe their legs and feet before donning the pants and
shoes, then coming on to squat all day on the store gallery eating cheese and crackers and peppermint candy
(bought on credit too out of Compson's and Ratcliffe's
showcase) and now not only they but Habersham and
Holston and Grenier too were there on sufferance,
anachronistic and alien, not really an annoyance yet but
simply a discomfort;

Then they were gone; the jail watched that: the halted
ungreased unpainted wagon, the span of underfed mules
attached to it by fragments of Eastern harness supple-
mented by raw deer-hide thongs, the nine young men—
the wild men, tameless and proud, who even in their own
generation's memory had been free and, in that of their

fathers, the heirs of kings—squatting about it, waiting, quiet and composed, not even dressed in the ancient forest-softened deerskins of their freedom but in the formal regalia of the white man's inexplicable ritualistic sabbaticals: broadcloth trousers and white shirts with boiled-starch bosoms (because they were traveling now; they would be visible to outworld, to strangers:—and carrying the New England-made shoes under their arms too since the distance would be long and walking was better barefoot), the shirts collarless and cravatless true enough and with the tails worn outside, but still board-rigid, gleaming, pristine, and in the rocking chair in the wagon, beneath the slave-borne parasol, the fat shapeless old matriarch in the regal sweat-stained purple silk and the plumed hat, barefoot too of course but, being a queen, with another slave to carry her slippers, putting her cross to the paper and then driving on, vanishing slowly and terrifically to the slow and terrific creak and squeak of the ungreased wagon—apparently and apparently only, since in reality it was as though, instead of putting an inked cross at the foot of a sheet of paper, she had lighted the train of a mine set beneath a dam, a dyke, a barrier already straining, bulging, bellying, not only towering over the land but leaning, looming, imminent with collapse, so that it only required the single light touch of the pen in that brown illiterate hand, and the wagon did not vanish slowly and terrifically from the scene to the terrific sound of its ungreased wheels, but was swept, hurled, flung not only out of Yoknapatawpha

County and Mississippi but the United States too, immobile and intact—the wagon, the mules, the rigid
shapeless old Indian woman and the nine heads which
surrounded her—like a float or a piece of stage property
dragged rapidly into the wings across the very backdrop
and amid the very bustle of the property-men setting up
for the next scene and act before the curtain had even
had time to fall;

There was no time; the next act and scene itself clearing
its own stage without waiting for property-men; or
rather, not even bothering to clear the stage but com-
mencing the new act and scene right in the midst of the
phantoms, the fading wraiths of that old time which had
been exhausted, used up, to be no more and never return: as though the mere and simple orderly ordinary
succession of days was not big enough, comprised not
scope enough, and so weeks and months and years had to
be condensed and compounded into one burst, one surge,
one soundless roar filled with one word: town: city: with
a name: Jefferson; men's mouths and their incredulous
faces (faces to which old Alex Holston had long since
ceased trying to give names or, for that matter, even to
recognise) were filled with it; that was only yesterday,
and by tomorrow the vast bright rush and roar had swept
the very town one block south, leaving in the tideless
backwater of an alley on a side-street the old jail which,
like the old mirror, had already looked at too much too
long, or like the patriarch who, whether or not he de-

creed the conversion of the mud-chinked cabin into a
mansion, had at least foreseen it, is now not only content
but even prefers the old chair on the back gallery, free
of the rustle of blueprints and the uproar of bickering
architects in the already dismantled living-room;

It (the old jail) didn't care, tideless in that backwash,
insulated by that city block of space from the turmoil of
the town's birthing, the mud-chinked log walls even car-
cerant of the flotsam of an older time already on its rapid
way out too: an occasional runaway slave or drunken
Indian or shoddy would-be heir of the old tradition of
Mason or Hare or Harpe (biding its time until, the
courthouse finished, the jail too would be translated into
brick, but, unlike the courthouse, merely a veneer of
brick, the old mud-chinked logs of the ground floor still
intact behind the patterned and symmetric sheath);
no longer even watching now, merely cognizant, remembering: only yesterday was a wilderness ordinary, a
store, a smithy, and already today was not a town, a
city, but the town and city: named; not a courthouse
but *the* courthouse, rising surging like the fixed blast of
a rocket, not even finished yet but already looming,
beacon focus and lodestar, already taller than anything
else, out of the rapid and fading wilderness—not the
wilderness receding from the rich and arable fields as
tide recedes, but rather the fields themselves, rich and
inexhaustible to the plow, rising sunward and airward
out of swamp and morass, themselves thrusting back and

down brake and thicket, bayou and bottom and forest, along with the copeless denizens—the wild men and animals—which once haunted them, wanting, dreaming, imagining, no other—lodestar and pole, drawing the people—the men and women and children, the maidens, the marriageable girls and the young men, flowing, pouring in with their tools and goods and cattle and slaves and gold money, behind ox- or mule-teams, by steamboat up Ikkemotubbe's old river from the Mississippi; only yesterday Pettigrew's pony express had been displaced by a stage-coach, yet already there was talk of a railroad less than a hundred miles to the north, to run all the way from Memphis to the Atlantic Ocean;

Going fast now: only seven years, and not only was the courthouse finished, but the jail too: not a new jail of course but the old one veneered over with brick, into two storeys, with white trim and iron-barred windows: only its face lifted, because behind the veneer were still the old ineradicable bones, the old ineradicable remembering: the old logs immured intact and lightless between the tiered symmetric bricks and the whitewashed plaster, immune now even to having to look, see, watch that new time which in a few years more would not even remember that the old logs were there behind the brick or had ever been, an age from which the drunken Indian had vanished, leaving only the highwayman, who had wagered his liberty on his luck, and the runaway nigger who, having no freedom to stake, had wagered merely

his milieu; that rapid, that fast: Sutpen's untameable
Paris architect long since departed, vanished (one
hoped) back to wherever it was he had made that aborted
midnight try to regain and had been overtaken and
caught in the swamp, not (as the town knew now) by
Sutpen and Sutpen's wild West Indian headman and Sutpen's bear hounds, nor even by Sutpen's destiny nor even
by his (the architect's) own, but by that of the town: the
long invincible arm of Progress itself reaching into that
midnight swamp to pluck him out of that bayed circle
of dogs and naked Negroes and pine torches, and
stamped the town with him like a rubber signature and
then released him, not flung him away like a squeezed-
out tube of paint, but rather (inattentive too) merely
opening its fingers, its hand; stamping his (the architect's) imprint not on just the courthouse and the jail,
but on the whole town, the flow and trickle of his bricks
never even faltering, his molds and kilns building the
two churches and then that Female Academy a certificate
from which, to a young woman of North Mississippi or
West Tennessee, would presently have the same mystic
significance as an invitation dated from Windsor castle
and signed by Queen Victoria would for a young female
from Long Island or Philadelphia;

That fast now: tomorrow, and the railroad did run unbroken from Memphis to Carolina, the light-wheeled
bulb-stacked wood-burning engines shrieking among the
swamps and cane-brakes where bear and panther still

lurked, and through the open woods where browsing deer still drifted in pale bands like unwinded smoke: because they—the wild animals, the beasts—remained, they coped, they would endure; a day, and they would flee, lumber, scuttle across the clearings already overtaken and relinquished by the hawk-shaped shadows of mail planes; they would endure, only the wild men were gone; indeed, tomorrow, and there would be grown men in Jefferson who could not even remember a drunken Indian in the jail; another tomorrow—so quick, so rapid, so fast—and not even a highwayman any more of the old true sanguinary girth and tradition of Hare and Mason and the mad Harpes; even Murrell, their thrice-compounded heir and apotheosis, who had taken his heritage of simple rapacity and bloodlust and converted it into a bloody dream of outlaw-empire, was gone, finished, as obsolete as Alexander, checkmated and stripped not even by man but by Progress, by a pierceless front of middle-class morality, which refused him even the dignity of execution as a felon, but instead merely branded him on the hand like an Elizabethan pickpocket—until all that remained of the old days for the jail to incarcerate was the runaway slave, for his little hour more, his little minute yet while the time, the land, the nation, the American earth, whirled faster and faster toward the plunging precipice of its destiny;

That fast, that rapid: a commodity in the land now which until now had dealt first in Indians: then in acres and

sections and boundaries:—an economy: Cotton: a king:
omnipotent and omnipresent: a destiny of which (obvious now) the plow and the axe had been merely the
tools; not plow and axe which had effaced the wilderness,
but Cotton: petty globules of Motion weightless and
myriad even in the hand of a child, incapable even of
wadding a rifle, let alone of charging it, yet potent
enough to sever the very taproots of oak and hickory and
gum, leaving the acre-shading tops to wither and vanish
in one single season beneath that fierce minted glare; not
the rifle nor the plow which drove at last the bear and
deer and panther into the last jungle fastnesses of the
river bottoms, but Cotton; not the soaring cupola of the
courthouse drawing people into the country, but that
same white tide sweeping them in: that tender skim
covering the winter's brown earth, burgeoning through
spring and summer into September's white surf crashing against the flanks of gin and warehouse and ringing
like bells on the marble counters of the banks: altering
not just the face of the land, but the complexion of the
town too, creating its own parasitic aristocracy not only
behind the columned porticoes of the plantation houses,
but in the counting-rooms of merchants and bankers and
the sanctums of lawyers, and not only these last, but
finally nadir complete: the county offices too: of sheriff
and tax-collector and bailiff and turnkey and clerk;
doing overnight to the old jail what Sutpen's architect
with all his brick and iron smithwork, had not been able
to accomplish—the old jail which had been unavoidable,

a necessity, like a public comfort-station, and which, like
the public comfort-station, was not ignored but simply
by mutual concord, not seen, not looked at, not named
by its purpose and aim, yet which to the older people of
the town, in spite of Sutpen's architect's face-lifting, was
still the old jail—now translated into an integer, a move-
able pawn on the county's political board like the sheriff's star or the clerk's bond or the bailiff's wand of
office; converted indeed. now, elevated (an apotheosis)
ten feet above the level of the town, so that the old buried
log walls now contained the living-quarters for the turnkey's family and the kitchen from which his wife catered,
at so much a meal, to the city's and the county's prisoners
—perquisite not for work or capability for work, but
for political fidelity and the numerality of votable kin by
blood or marriage—a jailor or turnkey, himself someone's cousin and with enough other cousins and inlaws
of his own to have assured the election of sheriff or
chancery- or circuit-clerk—a failed farmer who was
not at all the victim of his time but, on the contrary, was
its master, since his inherited and inescapable incapacity
to support his family by his own efforts had matched
him with an era and a land where government was
founded on the working premise of being primarily an
asylum for ineptitude and indigence, for the private
business failures among your or your wife's kin whom
otherwise you yourself would have to support—so much
his destiny's master that, in a land and time where a
man's survival depended not only on his ability to drive
a straight furrow and to fell a tree without maiming or

destroying himself, that fate had supplied to him one
child: a frail anemic girl with narrow workless hands
lacking even the strength to milk a cow, and then capped
its own vanquishment and eternal subjugation by the
paradox of giving him for his patronymic the designation of the vocation at which he was to fail: Farmer; this
was the incumbent, the turnkey, the jailor; the old tough
logs which had known Ikkemotubbe's drunken Chickasaws and brawling teamsters and trappers and flatboat-
men (and—for that one short summer night—the four
highwaymen, one of whom might have been the murderer,
Wiley Harpe), were now the bower framing a window
in which mused hour after hour and day and month and
year, the frail blonde girl not only incapable of (or at
least excused from) helping her mother cook, but even
of drying the dishes after her mother (or father perhaps)
washed them—musing, not even waiting for anyone or
anything, as far as the town knew, not even pensive, as
far as the town knew: just musing amid her blonde hair
in the window facing the country town street, day after
day and month after month and—as the town remembered it—year after year for what must have been three
or four of them, inscribing at some moment the fragile
and indelible signature of her meditation in one of the
panes of it (the window): her frail and workless name,
scratched by a diamond ring in her frail and workless
hand, and the date: *Cecilia Farmer April 16th 1861;*

At which moment the destiny of the land, the nation, the
South, the State, the County, was already whirling into

the plunge of its precipice, not that the State and the South knew it, because the first seconds of fall always seem like soar: a weightless deliberation preliminary to a rush not downward but upward, the falling body reversed during that second by transubstantiation into the upward rush of earth; a soar, an apex, the South's own apotheosis of its destiny and its pride, Mississippi and Yoknapatawpha County not last in this, Mississippi among the first of the eleven to ratify secession, the regiment of infantry which John Sartoris raised and organised with Jefferson for its headquarters, going to Virginia numbered Two in the roster of Mississippi regiments, the jail watching that too but just by cognizance from a block away: that noon, the regiment not even a regiment yet but merely a voluntary association of untried men who knew they were ignorant and hoped they were brave, the four sides of the Square lined with their fathers or grandfathers and their mothers and wives and sisters and sweethearts, the only uniform present yet that one in which Sartoris stood with his virgin sabre and his pristine colonel's braid on the courthouse balcony, bareheaded too while the Baptist minister prayed and the Richmond mustering officer swore the regiment in; and then (the regiment) gone; and now not only the jail but the town too hung without motion in a tideless backwash: the plunging body advanced far enough now into space as to have lost all sense of motion, weightless and immobile upon the light pressure of invisible air, gone now all diminishment of the precipice's lip, all increment

of the vast increaseless earth: a town of old men and
women and children and an occasional wounded soldier
(John Sartoris himself, deposed from his colonelcy by
a regimental election after Second Manassas, came home
and oversaw the making and harvesting of a crop on his
plantation before he got bored and gathered up a small
gang of irregular cavalry and carried it up into Tennessee to join Forrest), static in *quo*, rumored, mur-
mured of war only as from a great and incredible
dreamy distance, like far summer thunder: until the
spring of '64, the once-vast fixed impalpable increaseless
and threatless earth now one omnivorous roar of rock
(a roar so vast and so spewing, flinging ahead of itself,
like the spray above the maelstrom, the preliminary
anesthetic of shock so that the agony of bone and flesh
will not even be felt, as to contain and sweep along with
it the beginning, the first ephemeral phase, of this story,
permitting it to boil for an instant to the surface like a
chip or a twig—a match-stick or a bubble, say, too
weightless to give resistance for destruction to func-
tion against: in this case, a bubble, a minute globule
which was its own impunity, since what it—the bubble—
contained, having no part in rationality and being contemptuous of fact, was immune even to the rationality of
rock)—a sudden battle centering around Colonel Sartoris's plantation house four miles to the north, the line
of a creek held long enough for the main Confederate
body to pass through Jefferson to a stronger line on the
river heights south of the town, a rear-guard action of

cavalry in the streets of the town itself (and this was the story, the beginning of it; all of it too, the town might have been justified in thinking, presuming they had had time to see, notice, remark and then remember, even that little)—the rattle and burst of pistols, the hooves, the dust, the rush and scurry of a handful of horsemen led by a lieutenant, up the street past the jail, and the two of them—the frail and useless girl musing in the blonde mist of her hair beside the window-pane where three or four (or whatever it was) years ago she had inscribed with her grandmother's diamond ring her paradoxical and significantless name (and where, so it seemed to the town, she had been standing ever since), and the soldier, gaunt and tattered, battle-grimed and fleeing and undefeated, looking at one another for that moment across the fury and pell mell of battle;

Then gone; that night the town was occupied by Federal troops; two nights later, it was on fire (the Square, the stores and shops and the professional offices), gutted (the courthouse too), the blackened jagged topless jumbles of brick wall enclosing like a ruined jaw the blackened shell of the courthouse between its two rows of topless columns, which (the columns) were only blackened and stained, being tougher than fire: but not the jail, it escaped, untouched, insulated by its windless backwater from fire; and now the town was as though insulated by fire or perhaps cauterised by fire from fury and turmoil, the long roar of the rushing omnivorous

rock fading on to the east with the fading uproar of
the battle: and so in effect it was a whole year in
advance of Appomattox (only the undefeated unde-
featable women, vulnerable only to death, resisted,
endured, irreconcilable); already, before there was
a name for them (already their prototype before they
even existed as a species), there were carpetbaggers
in Jefferson—a Missourian named Redmond, a cotton-
and quartermaster-supplies speculator, who had followed
the Northern army to Memphis in '61 and (nobody knew
exactly how or why) had been with (or at least on the
fringe of) the military household of the brigadier commanding the force which occupied Jefferson, himself—
Redmond—going no farther, stopping, staying, none
knew the why for that either, why he elected Jefferson,
chose that alien fire-gutted site (himself one, or at least
the associate, of them who had set the match) to be his
future home; and a German private, a blacksmith, a
deserter from a Pennsylvania regiment, who appeared
in the summer of '64, riding a mule, with (so the tale
told later, when his family of daughters had become
matriarchs and grandmothers of the town's new aristocracy) for saddle-blanket sheaf on sheaf of virgin and
uncut United States banknotes, so Jefferson and Yoknapatawpha County had mounted Golgotha and passed beyond Appomattox a full year in advance, with returned
soldiers in the town, not only the wounded from the battle
of Jefferson, but whole men: not only the furloughed
from Forrest in Alabama and Johnston in Georgia and

Lee in Virginia, but the stragglers, the unmaimed flotsam and refuse of that single battle now drawing its final
constricting loop from the Atlantic Ocean at Old Point
Comfort, to Richmond: to Chattanooga: to Atlanta: to
the Atlantic Ocean again at Charleston, who were not
deserters but who could not rejoin any still-intact Confederate unit for the reason that there were enemy
armies between, so that in the almost faded twilight of
that land, the knell of Appomattox made no sound; when
in the spring and early summer of '65 the formally and
officially paroled and disbanded soldiers began to trickle
back into the county, there was anticlimax; they returned to a land which not only had passed through Appomattox over a year ago, it had had that year in which to
assimilate it, that whole year in which not only to ingest
surrender but (begging the metaphor, the figure) to con-
vert, metabolise it, and then defecate it as fertilizer for
the four-years' fallow land they were already in train
to rehabilitate a year before the Virginia knell rang the
formal change, the men of '65 returning to find themselves alien in the very land they had been bred and born
in and had fought for four years to defend, to find a
working and already solvent economy based on the
premise that it could get along without them; (and now
the rest of this story, since it occurs, happens, here: not
yet June in '65; this one had indeed wasted no time
getting back: a stranger, alone; the town did not even
know it had ever seen him before, because the other time
was a year ago and had lasted only while he galloped

through it firing a pistol backward at a Yankee army,
and he had been riding a horse—a fine though a little too
small and too delicate blooded mare—where now he
rode a big mule, which for that reason—its size—was a
better mule than the horse was a horse, but it was still a
mule, and of course the town could not know that he had
swapped the mare for the mule on the same day that he
traded his lieutenant's sabre—he still had the pistol—
for the stocking full of seed corn he had seen growing
in a Pennsylvania field and had not let even the mule
have one mouthful of it during the long journey across
the ruined land between the Atlantic seaboard and the
Jefferson jail, riding up to the jail at last, still gaunt and
tattered and dirty and still undefeated and not fleeing now
but instead making or at least planning a single-handed
assault against what any rational man would have considered insurmountable odds ((but then, that bubble had
ever been immune to the ephemerae of facts)); perhaps,
probably—without doubt: apparently she had been
standing leaning musing in it for three or four years in
1864; nothing had happened since, not in a land which
had even anticipated Appomattox, capable of shaking a
meditation that rooted, that durable, that veteran—the
girl watched him get down and tie the mule to the fence,
and perhaps while he walked from the fence to the door
he even looked for a moment at her, though possibly, perhaps even probably, not, since she was not his immediate
object now, he was not really concerned with her at the
moment, because he had so little time, he had none,

really: still to reach Alabama and the small hill farm which had been his father's and would now be his, if— no, when—he could get there, and it had not been ruined by four years of war and neglect, and even if the land was still plantable, even if he could start planting the stocking of corn tomorrow, he would be weeks and even months late; during that walk to the door and as he lifted his hand to knock on it, he must have thought with a kind of weary and indomitable outrage of how, already months late, he must still waste a day or maybe even two or three of them before he could load the girl onto the mule behind him and head at last for Alabama—this, at a time when of all things he would require patience and a clear head, trying for them ((courtesy too, which would be demanded now)), patient and urgent and polite, undefeated, trying to explain, in terms which they could understand or at least accept, his simple need and the urgency of it, to the mother and father whom he had never seen before and whom he never intended, or any- way anticipated, to see again, not that he had anything for or against them either: he simply intended to be too busy for the rest of his life, once they could get on the mule and start for home; not seeing the girl then, dur- ing the interview, not even asking to see her for a mo- ment when the interview was over, because he had to get the license now and then find the preacher: so that the first word he ever spoke to her was a promise delivered through a stranger; it was probably not until they were on the mule—the frail useless hands whose only strength

seemed to be that sufficient to fold the wedding license
into the bosom of her dress and then cling to the belt
around his waist—that he looked at her again or ((both
of them)) had time to learn one another's middle
name);

That was the story, the incident, ephemeral of an afternoon in late May, unrecorded by the town and the county
because they had little time too: which (the county and
the town) had anticipated Appomattox and kept that
lead, so that in effect Appomattox itself never over-
hauled them; it was the long pull of course, but they
had—as they would realise later—that priceless, that
unmatchable year; on New Year's Day, 1865, while the
rest of the South sat staring at the northeast horizon beyond which Richmond lay, like a family staring at the
closed door to a sick-room, Yoknapatawpha County was
already nine months gone in reconstruction; by New
Year's of '66, the gutted walls (the rain of two winters
had washed them clean of the smoke and soot) of the
Square had been temporarily roofed and were stores and
shops and offices again, and they had begun to restore
the courthouse: not temporary, this, but restored, exactly
as it had been, between the two columned porticoes, one
north and one south, which had been tougher than dynamite and fire, because it was the symbol: the County and
the City: and they knew how, who had done it before;
Colonel Sartoris was home now, and General Compson,
the first Jason's son, and though a tragedy had happened

to Sutpen and his pride—a failure not of his pride nor
even of his own bones and flesh, but of the lesser bones
and flesh which he had believed capable of supporting
the edifice of his dream—they still had the old plans of
his architect and even the architect's molds, and even
more: money, (strangely, curiously) Redmond, the
town's domesticated carpetbagger, symbol of a blind
rapacity almost like a biological instinct, destined to
cover the South like a migration of locusts; in the case
of this man, arriving a full year before its time and now
devoting no small portion of the fruit of his rapacity to
restoring the very building the destruction of which had
rung up the curtain for his appearance on the stage, had
been the formal visa on his passport to pillage; and by
New Year's of '76, this same Redmond with his money
and Colonel Sartoris and General Compson had built a
railroad from Jefferson north into Tennessee to connect
with the one from Memphis to the Atlantic Ocean; nor
content there either, north or south: another ten years
(Sartoris and Redmond and Compson quarreled, and
Sartoris and Redmond bought—probably with Redmond's money—Compson's interest in the railroad, and
the next year Sartoris and Redmond had quarreled and
the year after that, because of simple physical fear, Redmond killed Sartoris from ambush on the Jefferson
Square and fled, and at last even Sartoris's supporters—
he had no friends: only enemies and frantic admirers—
began to understand the result of that regimental election in the fall of '62) and the railroad was a part of that

system covering the whole South and East like the veins
in an oak leaf and itself mutually adjunctive to the other
intricate systems covering the rest of the United States,
so that you could get on a train in Jefferson now and, by
changing and waiting a few times, go anywhere in North
America;

No more into the United States, but into the *rest* of the
United States, because the long pull was over now; only
the aging unvanquished women were unreconciled, irreconcilable, reversed and irrevocably reverted against
the whole moving unanimity of panorama until, old
unordered vacant pilings above a tide's flood, they
themselves had an illusion of motion, facing irreconcil-
ably backward toward the old lost battles, the old
aborted cause, the old four ruined years whose very
physical scars ten and twenty and twenty-five changes of
season had annealed back into the earth; twenty-five and
then thirty-five years; not only a century and an age, but
a way of thinking died; the town itself wrote the epilogue
and epitaph: 1900, on Confederate Decoration Day,
Mrs. Virginia Depre, Colonel Sartoris's sister, twitched
a lanyard and the spring-restive bunting collapsed and
flowed, leaving the marble effigy—the stone infantryman
on his stone pedestal on the exact spot where forty years
ago the Richmond officer and the local Baptist minister
had mustered in the Colonel's regiment, and the old men
in the gray and braided coats (all officers now, none less
in rank than captain) tottered into the sunlight and fired

ᴈhotguns at the bland sky and raised their cracked
quavering voices in the shrill hackle-lifting yelling
which Lee and Jackson and Longstreet and the two John-
stons (and Grant and Sherman and Hooker and Pope
and McClellan and Burnside too for the matter of that)
had listened to amid the smoke and the din; epilogue
and epitaph, because apparently neither the U.D.C.
ladies who instigated and bought the monument, nor the
architect who designed it nor the masons who erected
it, had noticed that the marble eyes under the shading
marble palm stared not toward the north and the enemy,
but toward the south, toward (if anything) his own
rear—looking perhaps, the wits said (could say now,
with the old war thirty-five years past and you could
even joke about it—except the women, the ladies, the
unsurrendered, the irreconcilable, who even after another thirty-five years would still get up and stalk out of
picture houses showing *Gone With the Wind*), for rein-
forcements; or perhaps not a combat soldier at all, but
a provost marshal's man looking for deserters, or perhaps himself for a safe place to run to: because that old
war was dead; the sons of those tottering old men in gray
had already died in blue coats in Cuba, the macabre
mementos and testimonials and shrines of the new war
already usurping the earth before the blasts of blank
shotgun shells and the weightless collapsing of bunting
had unveiled the final ones to the old;

Not only a new century and a new way of thinking, but
of acting and behaving too: now you could go to bed in

a train in Jefferson and wake up tomorrow morning in New Orleans or Chicago; there were electric lights and running water in almost every house in town except the cabins of Negroes; and now the town bought and brought from a great distance a kind of gray crushed ballast-stone called macadam, and paved the entire street between the depot and the hotel, so that no more would the train-meeting hacks filled with drummers and lawyers and court-witnesses need to lurch and heave and strain through the winter mud-holes; every morning a wagon came to your very door with artificial ice and put it in your icebox on the back gallery for you, the children in rotational neighborhood gangs following it (the wagon), eating the fragments of ice which the Negro driver chipped off for them; and that summer a specially-built sprinkling-cart began to make the round of the streets each day; a new time, a new age: there were screens in windows now; people (white people) could actually sleep in summer night air, finding it harmless, uninimical: as though there had waked suddenly in man (or anyway in his womenfolks) a belief in his inalienable civil right to be free of dust and bugs;

Moving faster and faster: from the speed of two horses on either side of a polished tongue, to that of thirty then fifty then a hundred under a tin bonnet no bigger than a wash-tub: which from almost the first explosion, would have to be controlled by police; already in a back yard on the edge of town, an ex-blacksmith's-apprentice, a grease-covered man with the eyes of a visionary monk, was building a gasoline buggy, casting and boring his own cylinders and rods and cams, inventing his own coils and plugs and valves as he found he needed them, which would run, and did: crept popping and stinking out of the alley at the exact moment when the banker Bayard Sartoris, the Colonel's son, passed in his carriage: as a result of which, there is on the books of Jefferson today a law prohibiting the operation of any mechanically-propelled vehicle on the streets of the corporate town: who (the same banker Sartoris) died in one (such was progress, that fast, that rapid) lost from control on an icy road by his (the banker's) grandson, who had just returned from (such was progress) two years of service as a combat airman on the Western Front and now the camouflage paint is weathering slowly from a French point-seventy-five field piece squatting on one flank of the base of the Confederate monument, but even before it faded there was neon in the town and A.A.A. and C.C.C. in the county, and W.P.A. ("and XYZ and etc.," as "Uncle Pete" Gombault, a lean clean tobacco-chewing old man, incumbent of a political sinecure under the designation of United States marshal —an office held back in reconstruction times, when the State of Mississippi was a United States military district, by a Negro man who was still living in 1925—firemaker, sweeper, janitor and furnace-attendant to five or six lawyers and doctors and one of the banks—and still known as "Mulberry" from the avocation which he had followed before and during and after his incumbency as

marshal: peddling illicit whiskey in pint and half-pint
bottles from a cache beneath the roots of a big mulberry
tree behind the drugstore of his pre-1865 owner—put
it) in both; W.P.A. and XYZ marking the town and the
county as war itself had not: gone now were the last of
the forest trees which had followed the shape of the
Square, shading the unbroken second-storey balcony
onto which the lawyers' and doctors' offices had opened,
which shaded in its turn the fronts of the stores and the
walkway beneath; and now was gone even the balcony itself with its wrought-iron balustrade on which in the
long summer afternoons the lawyers would prop their
feet to talk; and the continuous iron chain looping from
wooden post to post along the circumference of the courthouse yard, for the farmers to hitch their teams to; and
the public watering trough where they could water them,
because gone was the last wagon to stand on the Square
during the spring and summer and fall Saturdays and
trading-days, and not only the Square but the streets
leading into it were paved now, with fixed signs of inter-
diction and admonition applicable only to something
capable of moving faster than thirty miles an hour; and
now the last forest tree was gone from the courthouse
yard too, replaced by formal synthetic shrubs contrived
and schooled in Wisconsin greenhouses, and in the
courthouse (the city hall too) a courthouse and city hall
gang, in miniature of course (but that was not its fault
but the fault of the city's and the county's size and population and wealth) but based on the pattern of Chicago

and Kansas City and Boston and Philadelphia (and
which, except for its minuscularity, neither Philadelphia
nor Boston nor Kansas City nor Chicago need have
blushed at) which every three or four years would try
again to raze the old courthouse in order to build a new
one, not that they did not like the old one nor wanted the
new, but because the new one would bring into the town
and county that much more increment of unearned federal money;

And now the paint is preparing to weather from an anti-
tank howitzer squatting on rubber tires on the opposite
flank of the Confederate monument; and gone now from
the fronts of the stores are the old brick made of native
clay in Sutpen's architect's old molds, replaced now by
sheets of glass taller than a man and longer than a wagon
and team, pressed intact in Pittsburgh factories and
framing interiors bathed now in one shadowless corpse-
glare of fluorescent light; and, now and at last, the last
of silence too: the county's hollow inverted air one
resonant boom and ululance of radio: and thus no more
Yoknapatawpha's air nor even Mason and Dixon's air,
but America's: the patter of comedians, the baritone
screams of female vocalists, the babbling pressure to
buy and buy and still buy arriving more instantaneous
than light, two thousands miles from New York and Los
Angeles; one air, one nation: the shadowless fluorescent
corpse-glare bathing the sons and daughters of men and
women, Negro and white both, who were born to and who

passed all their lives in denim overalls and calico, haggling by cash or the installment-plan for garments copied last week out of *Harper's Bazaar* or *Esquire* in East Side sweat-shops: because an entire generation of farmers has vanished, not just from Yoknapatawpha's but from Mason and Dixon's earth: the self-consumer: the machine which displaced the man because the exodus of the man left no one to drive the mule, now that the machine was threatening to extinguish the mule; time was when the mule stood in droves at daylight in the plantation mule-lots across the plantation road from the serried identical ranks of two-room shotgun shacks in which lived in droves with his family the Negro tenant- or share- or furnish-hand who bridled him (the mule) in the lot at sunup and followed him through the plumb-straight monotony of identical furrows and back to the lot at sundown, with (the man) one eye on where the mule was going and the other eye on his (the mule's) heels; both gone now: the one, to the last of the forty- and fifty- and sixty-acre hill farms inaccessible from unmarked dirt roads, the other to New York and Detroit and Chicago and Los Angeles ghettos, or nine out of ten of him that is, the tenth one mounting from the handles of a plow to the springless bucket seat of a tractor, dispossessing and displacing the other nine just as the tractor had dispossessed and displaced the other eighteen mules to whom that nine would have been complement; then Warsaw and Dunkerque displaced that tenth in his turn, and now the planter's not-yet-drafted son drove the tractor: and then Pearl Harbor and Tobruk and Utah Beach displaced that son, leaving the planter himself on the seat of the tractor, for a little while that is—or so he thought, forgetting that victory or defeat both are bought at the same exorbitant price of change and alteration; one nation, one world: young men who had never been farther from Yoknapatawpha County than Memphis or New Orleans (and that not often), now talked glibly of street intersections in Asiatic and European capitals, returning no more to inherit the long monotonous endless unendable furrows of Mississippi cotton fields, living now (with now a wife and next year a wife and child and the year after that a wife and children) in automobile trailers or G.I. barracks on the outskirts of liberal arts colleges, and the father and now grandfather himself still driving the tractor across the gradually diminishing fields between the long looping skeins of electric lines bringing electric power from the Appalachian mountains, and the subterrene steel veins bringing the natural gas from the Western plains, to the little lost lonely farmhouses glittering and gleaming with automatic stoves and washing machines and television antennae;

One nation: no longer anywhere, not even in Yoknapatawpha County, one last irreconcilable fastness of stronghold from which to enter the United States, because at last even the last old sapless indomitable unvanquished widow or maiden aunt had died and the old deathless Lost Cause had become a faded (though still

select) social club or caste, or form of behavior when
you remembered to observe it on the occasions when
young men from Brooklyn, exchange students at Mississippi or Arkansas or Texas Universities, vended tiny
Confederate battle flags among the thronged Saturday
afternoon ramps of football stadia; one world: the tank
gun: captured from a regiment of Germans in an African
desert by a regiment of Japanese in American uniforms,
whose mothers and fathers at the time were in a California detention camp for enemy aliens, and carried
(the gun) seven thousand miles back to be set halfway
between, as a sort of secondary flying buttress to a
memento of Shiloh and The Wilderness; one universe,
one cosmos: contained in one America: one towering
frantic edifice poised like a card-house over the abyss of
the mortgaged generations; one boom, one peace: one
swirling rocket-roar filling the glittering zenith as with
golden feathers, until the vast hollow sphere of his air,
the vast and terrible burden beneath which he tries to
stand erect and lift his battered and indomitable head—
the very substance in which he lives and, lacking which,
he would vanish in a matter of seconds—is murmurous
with his fears and terrors and disclaimers and repudi-
ations and his aspirations and dreams and his baseless
hopes, bouncing back at him in radar waves from the
constellations;

And still—the old jail—endured, sitting in its rumorless
cul-de-sac, its almost seasonless backwater in the middle

of that rush and roar of civic progress and social alteration and change like a collarless (and reasonably clean:
merely dingy: with a day's stubble and no garters to his
socks) old man sitting in his suspenders and stocking
feet, on the back kitchen steps inside a walled courtyard;
actually not isolated by location so much as insulated by
obsolescence: on the way out of course (to disappear
from the surface of the earth along with the rest of the
town on the day when all America, after cutting down
all the trees and leveling the hills and mountains with
bulldozers, would have to move underground to make
room for, get out of the way of, the motor cars) but like
the track-walker in the tunnel, the thunder of the express
mounting behind him, who finds himself opposite a niche
or crack exactly his size in the wall's living and impregnable rock, and steps into it, inviolable and secure while
destruction roars past and on and away, grooved in-
eluctably to the spidery rails of its destiny and destination; not even—the jail—worth selling to the United
States for some matching allocation out of the federal
treasury; not even (so fast, so far, was Progress) any
more a real pawn, let alone knight or rook, on the
County's political board, not even plum in true worth
of the word: simply a modest sinecure for the husband
of someone's cousin, who had failed not as a father but
merely as a fourth-rate farmer or day-laborer;

It survived, endured; it had its inevictable place in the
town and the county; it was even still adding modestly

not just to its but to the town's and the county's history
too: somewhere behind that dingy brick façade, between
the old durable hand-molded brick and the cracked
creosote-impregnated plaster of the inside walls (though
few in the town or county any longer knew that they were
there) were the old notched and mortised logs which
(this, the town and county did remember; it was part of
its legend) had held someone who might have been Wiley
Harpe; during that summer of 1864, the federal brigadier who had fired the Square and the courthouse had
used the jail as his provost-marshal's guard-house; and
even children in high school remembered how the jail
had been host to the Governor of the State while he dis-
charged a thirty-day sentence for contempt of court for
refusing to testify in a paternity suit brought against one
of his lieutenants: but isolate, even its legend and record
and history, indisputable in authenticity yet a little
oblique, elliptic or perhaps just ellipsoid, washed thinly
over with a faint quiet cast of apocryphy: because there
were new people in the town now, strangers, outlanders,
living in new minute glass-walled houses set as neat and
orderly and antiseptic as cribs in a nursery ward, in new
subdivisions named Fairfield or Longwood or Halcyon
Acres which had once been the lawn or back yard or
kitchen garden of the old residences (the old obsolete
columned houses still standing among them like old
horses surged suddenly out of slumber in the middle of
a flock of sheep), who had never seen the jail; that is,
they had looked at it in passing, they knew where it was,

when their kin or friends or acquaintances from the East or North or California visited them or passed through Jefferson on the way to New Orleans or Florida, they could even repeat some of its legend or history to them: but they had had no contact with it; it was not a part of their lives; they had the automatic stoves and furnaces and milk deliveries and lawns the size of installment-plan rugs; they had never had to go to the jail on the morning after June tenth or July Fourth or Thanksgiving or Christmas or New Year's (or for that matter, on almost any Monday morning) to pay the fine of house-man or gardener or handyman so that he could hurry on home (still wearing his hangover or his barely-stanched razor-slashes) and milk the cow or clean the furnace or mow the lawn;

So only the old citizens knew the jail any more, not old people but old citizens: men and women old not in years but in the constancy of the town, or against that constancy, concordant (not coeval of course, the town's date was a century and a quarter ago now, but in accord against that continuation) with that thin durable continuity born a hundred and twenty-five years ago out of a handful of bandits captured by a drunken militia squad, and a bitter ironical incorruptible wilderness mail-rider, and a monster wrought-iron padlock—that steadfast and durable and unhurryable continuity against or across which the vain and glittering ephemerae of progress and alteration washed in substanceless repetitive evanescent scarless waves, like the wash and glare of the neon sign on what was still known as the Holston House diagonally opposite, which would fade with each dawn from the old brick walls of the jail and leave no trace; only the old citizens still knew it: the intractable and obsolescent of the town who still insisted on wood-burning ranges and cows and vegetable gardens and handymen who had to be taken out of hock on the mornings after Saturday nights and holidays; or the ones who actually spent the Saturday- and holiday-nights inside the barred doors and windows of the cells or bull-pen for drunkenness or fighting or gambling—the servants, housemen and gardeners and handymen, who would be extracted the next morning by their white folks, and the others (what the town knew as the New Negro, independent of that commodity) who would sleep there every night beneath the thin ruby checker-barred wash and fade of the hotel sign, while they worked their fines out on the street; and the County, since its cattle-thieves and moonshiners went to trial from there, and its murderers—by electricity now (so fast, that fast, was Progress)—to eternity from there; in fact it was still, not a factor perhaps, but at least an integer, a cipher, in the county's political establishment; at least still used by the Board of Supervisors, if not as a lever, at least as something like Punch's stuffed club, not intended to break bones, not aimed to leave any permanent scars;

So only the old knew it, the irreconcilable Jeffersonians and Yoknapatawphians who had (and without doubt firmly intended to continue to have) actual personal

dealings with it on the blue Monday mornings after holidays, or during the semi-yearly terms of Circuit or
Federal Court:—until suddenly you, a stranger, an outlander say from the East or the North or the Far West,
passing through the little town by simple accident, or
perhaps relation or acquaintance or friend of one of the
outland families which had moved into one of the pristine
and recent subdivisions, yourself turning out of your
way to fumble among road signs and filling stations out
of frank curiosity, to try to learn, comprehend, understand what had brought your cousin or friend or acquaintance to elect to live here—not specifically here, of
course, not specifically Jefferson, but such as here, such
as Jefferson—suddenly you would realise that something curious was happening or had happened here: that
instead of dying off as they should as time passed, it was
as though these old irreconcilables were actually increasing in number; as though with each interment of
one, two more shared that vacancy: where in 1900, only
thirty-five years afterward, there could not have been
more than two or three capable of it, either by knowledge or memory of leisure, or even simple willingness
and inclination, now, in 1951, eighty-six years afterward,
they could be counted in dozens (and in 1965, a hundred years afterward, in hundreds because—by now
you had already begun to understand why your kin or
friends or acquaintance had elected to come to such as
this with his family and call it his life—by then the
children of that second outland invasion following a

war, would also have become not just Mississippians but Jeffersonians and Yoknapatawphians: by which time—who knows?—not merely the pane, but the whole window, perhaps the entire wall, may have been removed and embalmed intact into a museum by an historical, or anyway a cultural, club of ladies—why, by that time, they may not even know, or even need to know: only that the window-pane bearing the girl's name and the date is that old, which is enough; has lasted that long: one small rectangle of wavy, crudely-pressed, almost opaque glass, bearing a few faint scratches apparently no more durable than the thin dried slime left by the passage of a snail, yet which has endured a hundred years) who are capable and willing too to quit whatever they happen to be doing—sitting on the last of the wooden benches beneath the last of the locust and chinaberry trees among the potted conifers of the new age dotting the courthouse yard, or in the chairs along the shady sidewalk before the Holston House, where a breeze always blows—to lead you across the street and into the jail and (with courteous neighborly apologies to the jailor's wife stirring or turning on the stove the peas and grits and side-meat—purchased in bargain-lot quantities by shrewd and indefatigable peditation from store to store—which she will serve to the prisoners for dinner or supper at so much a head—plate—payable by the County, which is no mean factor in the sinecure of her husband's incumbency) into the kitchen and so to the cloudy pane bearing the faint scratches which, after a moment, you will descry to be a name and a date;

Not at first, of course, but after a moment, a second, because at first you would be a little puzzled, a little impatient because of your illness-at-ease from having been dragged without warning or preparation into the private kitchen of a strange woman cooking a meal; you would think merely *What? So what?* annoyed and even a little outraged, until suddenly, even while you were thinking it, something has already happened: the faint frail illegible meaningless even inference-less scratching on the ancient poor-quality glass you stare at, has moved, under your eyes, even while you stared at it, coalesced, seeming actually to have entered into another sense than vision: a scent, a whisper, filling that hot cramped strange room already fierce with the sound and reek of frying pork-fat: the two of them in conjunction—the old milky obsolete glass, and the scratches on it: that tender ownerless obsolete girl's name and the old dead date in April almost a century ago—speaking, murmuring, back from, out of, across from, a time as old as lavender, older than album or stereopticon, as old as daguerreotype itself;

And being a stranger and a guest would have been enough, since, a stranger and a guest, you would have shown the simple courtesy and politeness of asking the questions naturally expected of you by the host or anyway volun-

teer guide, who had dropped whatever he was doing
(even if that had been no more than sitting with others
of his like on a bench in a courthouse yard or on the
sidewalk before a hotel) in order to bring you here; not
to mention your own perfectly natural desire for, not
revenge perhaps, but at least compensation, restitution,
vindication, for the shock and annoyance of having been
brought here without warning or preparation, into the
private quarters of a strange woman engaged in something as intimate as cooking a meal; but by now you had
not only already begun to understand why your kin or
friend or acquaintance had elected, not Jefferson but
such as Jefferson, for his life, but you had heard that
voice, that whisper, murmur, frailer than the scent of
lavender, yet (for that second anyway) louder than all
the seethe and fury of frying fat; so you ask the questions, not only which are expected of you, but whose
answers you yourself must have if you are to get back
into your car and fumble with any attention and con-
centration among the road signs and filling stations, to
get on to wherever it is you had started when you stopped
by chance or accident in Jefferson for an hour or a day
or a night, and the host—guide—answers them, to the
best of his ability out of the town's composite heritage
of remembering that long back, told, repeated, inherited
to him by his father; or rather, his mother: from her
mother: or better still, to him when he himself was a
child, direct from his great-aunt: the spinsters, maiden
and childless out of a time when there were too many

women because too many of the young men were maimed or dead: the indomitable and undefeated, maiden progenitresses of spinster and childless descendants still capable of rising up and stalking out in the middle of *Gone With the Wind*;

And again one sense assumes the office of two or three: not only hearing, listening, and seeing too, but you are even standing on the same spot, the same boards she did that day she wrote her name into the window and on the other one three years later watching and hearing through and beyond that faint fragile defacement the sudden rush and thunder: the dust: the crackle and splatter of pistols: then the face, gaunt, battle-dirty, stubbled-over; urgent of course, but merely harried, harassed; not defeated, turned for a fleeing instant across the turmoil and the fury, then gone: and still the girl in the window (the guide—host—has never said one or the other; without doubt in the town's remembering after a hundred years it has changed that many times from blonde to dark and back to blonde again: which doesn't matter, since in your own remembering that tender mist and vail will be forever blonde) not even waiting: musing; a year, and still not even waiting: meditant, not even unimpatient: just patienceless, in the sense that blindness and zenith are colorless; until at last the mule, not out of the long northeastern panorama of defeat and dust and fading smoke, but drawn out of it by that impregnable, that invincible, that incredible, that terrify-

ing passivity, coming at that one fatigueless unflagging
jog all the way from Virginia—the mule which was a
better mule in 1865 than the blood mare had been a
horse in '-2 and '-3 and '-4, for the reason that this was
now 1865, and the man, still gaunt and undefeated:
merely harried and urgent and short of time to get on to
Alabama and see the condition of his farm—or (for
that matter) if he still had a farm, and now the girl,
the fragile and workless girl not only incapable of milk-
ing a cow but of whom it was never even demanded, required, suggested, that she substitute for her father in
drying the dishes, mounting pillion on a mule behind a
paroled cavalry subaltern out of a surrendered army
who had swapped his charger for a mule and the sabre
of his rank and his defeatless pride for a stocking
full of seed corn, whom she had not known or even
spoken to long enough to have learned his middle name
or his preference in food, or told him hers, and no time
for that even now: riding, hurrying toward a country
she had never seen, to begin a life which was not even
simple frontier, engaged only with wilderness and shoe-
less savages and the tender hand of God, but one which
had been rendered into a desert (assuming that it was
still there at all to be returned to) by the iron and fire
of civilization;

Which was all your host (guide) could tell you, since
that was all he knew, inherited, inheritable from the
town: which was enough, more than enough in fact,

since all you needed was the face framed in its blonde and delicate vail behind the scratched glass; yourself, the stranger, the outlander from New England or the prairies or the Pacific Coast, no longer come by the chance or accident of kin or friend or acquaintance or roadmap, but drawn too from ninety years away by that incredible and terrifying passivity, watching in your turn through and beyond that old milk-dim disfigured glass that shape, that delicate frail and useless bone and flesh departing pillion on a mule without one backward look, to the reclaiming of an abandoned and doubtless even ravaged (perhaps even usurped) Alabama hill farm—being lifted onto the mule (the first time he touched her probably, except to put the ring on: not to prove nor even to feel, touch, if there actually was a girl under the calico and the shawls; there was no time for that yet; but simply to get her up so they could start), to ride a hundred miles to become the farmless mother of farmers (she would bear a dozen, all boys, herself no older, still fragile, still workless among the churns and stoves and brooms and stacks of wood which even a woman could split into kindlings; unchanged), bequeathing to them in their matronymic the heritage of that invincible inviolable ineptitude;

Then suddenly, you realise that that was nowhere near enough, not for that face—bridehood, motherhood, grandmotherhood, then widowhood and at last the grave —the long peaceful connubial progress toward matri-

archy in a rocking chair nobody else was allowed to sit
in, then a headstone in a country churchyard—not for
that passivity, that stasis, that invincible captaincy of
soul which didn't even need to wait but simply to be,
breathe tranquilly, and take food—infinite not only in
capacity but in scope too: that face, one maiden muse
which had drawn a man out of the running pell mell of a
cavalry battle, a whole year around the long iron per-
imeter of duty and oath, from Yoknapatawpha County,
Mississippi, across Tennessee into Virginia and up
to the fringe of Pennsylvania before it curved back into
its closing fade along the headwaters of the Appomattox
river and at last removed from him its iron hand: where,
a safe distance at last into the rainy woods from the
picket lines and the furled flags and the stacked muskets,
a handful of men leading spent horses, the still-warm
pistols still loose and quick for the hand in the un-
strapped scabbards, gathered in the failing twilight—
privates and captains, sergeants and corporals and sub-
alterns—talking a little of one last desperate cast southward where (by last report) Johnston was still intact,
knowing that they would not, that they were done not
only with vain resistance but with indomitability too;
already departed this morning in fact for Texas, the
West, New Mexico: a new land even if not yet (spent too
—like the horses—from the long harassment and anguish of remaining indomitable and undefeated) a new
hope, putting behind them for good and all the loss of
both: the young dead bride—drawing him (that face)

even back from this too, from no longer having to remain
undefeated too: who swapped the charger for the mule
and the sabre for the stocking of seed corn: back across
the whole ruined land and the whole disastrous year by
that virgin inevictable passivity more inescapable than
lodestar;

Not that face; that was nowhere near enough: no symbol
there of connubial matriarchy, but fatal instead with all
insatiate and deathless sterility; spouseless, barren, and
undescended; not even demanding more than that: simply
requiring it, requiring all—Lilith's lost and insatiable
face drawing the substance—the will and hope and
dream and imagination—of all men (you too: yourself
and the host too) into that one bright fragile net and
snare; not even to be caught, over-flung, by one single
unerring cast of it, but drawn to watch in patient and
thronging turn the very weaving of the strangling golden
strands—drawing the two of you from almost a hundred
years away in your turn—yourself the stranger, the outlander with a B.A. or (perhaps even) M.A. from Harvard
or Northwestern or Stanford, passing through Jefferson
by chance or accident on the way to somewhere else, and
the host who in three generations has never been out of
Yoknapatawpha further than a few prolonged Saturday
nights in Memphis or New Orleans, who has heard of
Jenny Lind, not because he has heard of Mark Twain
and Mark Twain spoke well of her, but for the same reason that Mark Twain spoke well of her: not that she sang

songs, but that she sang them in the old West in the old
days, and the man sanctioned by public affirmation to
wear a pistol openly in his belt is an inevictable part of
the Missouri and the Yoknapatawpha dream too, but
never of Duse or Bernhardt or Maximilian of Mexico,
let alone whether the Emperor of Mexico even ever had a
wife or not (saying—the host—: 'You mean, she was
one of them? maybe even that emperor's wife?' and
you: 'Why not? Wasn't she a Jefferson girl?')—to stand,
in this hot strange little room furious with frying fat,
among the roster and chronicle, the deathless murmur
of the sublime and deathless names and the deathless
faces, the faces omnivorous and insatiable and forever
incontent: demon-nun and angel-witch; empress, siren,
Erinys: Mistinguette, too, invincible possessed of a half-
century more of years than the mere three score or so she
bragged and boasted, for you to choose among, which
one she was—not *might* have been, nor even *could* have
been, but *was*: so vast, so limitless in capacity is man's
imagination to disperse and burn away the rubble-dross
of fact and probability, leaving only truth and dream—
then gone, you are outside again, in the hot noon sun:
late; you have already wasted too much time: to un-
fumble among the road signs and filling stations to get
back onto a highway you know, back into the United
States; not that it matters, since you know again now
that there is no time: no space: no distance: a fragile and
workless scratching almost depthless in a sheet of old
barely transparent glass, and (all you had to do was

look at it a while; all you have to do now is remember it) there is the clear undistanced voice as though out of the delicate antenna-skeins of radio, further than empress's throne, than splendid insatiation, even than matriarch's peaceful rocking chair, across the vast instantaneous intervention, from the long long time ago: *'Listen, stranger; this was myself: this was I.'*

Interior, the Jail. 10:30 A.M. March twelfth.

The common room, or 'bull-pen'. It is on the second floor. A heavy barred door at left is the entrance to it, to the entire cell-block, which—the cells—are indicated by a row of steel doors, each with its own individual small barred window, lining the right wall. A narrow passage at the far end of the right wall leads to more cells. A single big heavily barred window in the rear wall looks down into the street. It is mid-morning of a sunny day.

The door, left, opens with a heavy clashing of the steel lock, and swings back and outward. Temple enters, followed by Stevens and the Jailor. Temple has changed her dress, but wears the fur coat and the same hat. Stevens is dressed exactly as he was in Act Two. The Jailor is a typical small-town turnkey, in shirt-sleeves and no necktie, carrying the heavy keys on a big iron ring against his leg as a farmer carries a lantern, say. He is drawing the door to behind him as he enters.

Temple stops just inside the room. Stevens perforce stops also. The Jailor closes the door and locks it on the inside with another clash and clang of steel, and turns.

JAILOR

Well, Lawyer, singing school will be over after tonight, huh?

> (to Temple)

You been away, you see. You dont know about this, you aint up with what's—

> (he stops himself quickly; he is about to commit what he would call a very bad impoliteness, what in the tenets of his class and kind would be the most grave of gaucherie and bad taste: re-ferring directly to a recent bereavement in the presence of the bereaved, particularly one of this nature, even though by this time tomor-row the State itself will have made restitution with the perpetrator's life. He tries to rectify it)

Not that I wouldn't too, if I'd a been the ma of the very—

> (stopping himself again; this is getting worse than ever; now he not only is looking at Stevens, but actu-ally addressing him)

Every Sunday night, and every night since last Sunday except last night—come to think of it, Lawyer, where was you last night? We missed you—Lawyer here and Na—the prisoner have been singing hymns in her cell. The first time, he just stood out there on the sidewalk while she stood in that window yonder. Which was all right, not doing no harm, just singing church hymns. Because all of us home folks here in Jefferson and Yoknapatawpha County both know Lawyer Stevens, even if some of us might have thought he got a little out of line—

(again it is getting out of hand; he realises it, but there is nothing he can do now; he is like someone walking a foot-log: all he can do is move as fast as he dares until he can reach solid ground or at least pass another log to leap to)

defending a nigger murderer, let alone when it was his own niece was mur—

(and reaches another log and leaps to it without stopping: at least one running at right angles for a little distance into simple generality)

—maybe suppose some stranger say, some durn Yankee tourist, happened to be passing through in a car, when we get enough durn criticism from Yankees like it is—besides, a white man standing out there in the cold, while a durned nigger murderer is up here all warm and comfortable; so it happened that me and Mrs Tubbs hadn't went to prayer meeting that night, so we invited him to come in; and to tell the truth, we come to enjoy it too. Because as soon as they found out there wasn't going to be no objection to it, the other nigger prisoners (I got five more right now, but I taken them out back and locked them up in the coal house so you could have some privacy) joined in too, and by the second or third Sunday night, folks was stopping along the street to listen to them instead of going to regular church. Of course, the other niggers would just be in and out over Saturday and Sunday night for fighting or gambling or vagrance or drunk, so just about the time they would begin to get in tune, the whole choir would be a complete turnover. In fact, I had a idea at one time to have the Marshal comb the nigger dives and joints not for drunks and gamblers, but basses and baritones.

> (he starts to laugh, guffaws once, then catches himself; he looks at Temple with

> something almost gentle, al-
> most articulate, in his face,
> taking (as though) by the
> horns, facing frankly and
> openly the dilemma of his
> own inescapable vice)

Excuse me, Mrs Stevens. I talk too much. All I
want to say is, this whole county, not a man or
woman, wife or mother either in the whole state
of Mississippi, that dont—dont feel—

> (stopping again, looking at
> Temple)

There I am, still at it, still talking too much.
Wouldn't you like for Mrs Tubbs to bring you
up a cup of coffee or maybe a Coca-Cola? She's
usually got a bottle or two of sody pop in the
icebox.

TEMPLE

No, thank you, Mr Tubbs. If we could just see
Nancy—

JAILOR

> (turning)

Sure, sure.

He crosses toward the rear, right, and disappears into
the passage.

TEMPLE

The blindfold again. Out of a Coca-Cola bottle
this time or a cup of county-owned coffee.

Stevens takes the same pack of cigarettes from his overcoat pocket, though Temple has declined before he can
even offer them.

No, thanks. My hide's toughened now. I hardly
feel it. People. They're really innately, inherently gentle and compassionate and kind. That's
what wrings, wrenches . . . something. Your en-
trails, maybe. The member of the mob who holds
up the whole ceremony for seconds or even minutes while he dislodges a family of bugs or
lizards from the log he is about to put on the
fire—

> (there is the clash of another
> steel door off-stage as the
> Jailor unlocks Nancy's cell.
> Temple pauses, turns and
> listens, then continues rap-
> idly)

And now I've got to say 'I forgive you, sister'
to the nigger who murdered my baby. No: it's
worse: I've even got to transpose it, turn it
around. I've got to start off my new life being
forgiven again. How can I say that? Tell me.
How can I?

She stops again and turns farther as Nancy enters from the rear alcove, followed by the Jailor, who passes Nancy and comes on, carrying the ring of keys once more like a farmer's lantern.

JAILOR
(to Stevens)

Okay, Lawyer. How much time you want? Thirty minutes? an hour?

STEVENS

Thirty minutes should be enough.

JAILOR
(still moving toward the exit, left)

Okay.
(to Temple)

You sure you dont want that coffee or a Coca-Cola? I could bring you up a rocking chair—

TEMPLE

Thank you just the same, Mr Tubbs.

JAILOR

Okay.
(at the exit door, unlocking it)

Thirty minutes, then.

He unlocks the door, opens it, exits, closes and locks it behind him; the lock clashes, his footsteps die away. Nancy has slowed and stopped where the Jailor passed her; she now stands about six feet to the rear of Temple and Stevens. Her face is calm, unchanged. She is dressed exactly as before, except for the apron; she still wears the hat.

NANCY

(to Temple)

You been to California, they tell me. I used to think maybe I would get there too, some day. But I waited too late to get around to it.

TEMPLE

So did I. Too late and too long. Too late when I went to California, and too late when I came back. That's it: too late and too long, not only for you, but for me too; already too late when both of us should have got around to running, like from death itself, from the very air anybody breathed named Drake or Mannigoe.

NANCY

Only, we didnt. And you come back, yesterday evening. I heard that too. And I know where you were last night, you and him both.

(indicating Stevens)

You went to see the Mayor.

TEMPLE

Oh, God, the mayor. No: the Governor, the Big
Man himself, in Jackson. Of course; you knew
that as soon as you realised that Mr Gavin
wouldn't be here last night to help you sing,
didn't you? In fact, the only thing you cant
know about it is what the Governor told us. You
cant know that yet, no matter how clairvoyant
you are, because we—the Governor and Mr
Gavin and I—were not even talking about you;
the reason I—we had to go and see him was not
to beg or plead or bind or loose, but because it
would be my right, my duty, my privilege—
Dont look at me, Nancy.

NANCY

I'm not looking at you. Besides, it's all right. I
know what the Governor told you. Maybe I could
have told you last night what he would say, and
saved you the trip. Maybe I ought to have—sent
you the word as soon as I heard you were back
home, and knowed what you and him—

> (again she indicates Stevens
> with that barely discernible
> movement of her head, her
> hands still folded across her
> middle as though she still
> wore the absent apron)

—both would probably be up to. Only, I didn't.
But it's all right—

TEMPLE

Why didn't you? Yes, look at me. This is worse,
but the other is terrible.

NANCY

What?

TEMPLE

Why didn't you send me the word?

NANCY

Because that would have been hoping: the
hardest thing of all to break, get rid of, let go
of, the last thing of all poor sinning man will
turn aloose. Maybe it's because that's all he's
got. Leastways, he holds onto it, hangs onto it.
Even with salvation laying right in his hand, and
all he's got to do is, choose between it; even with
salvation already in his hand and all he needs is
just to shut his fingers, old sin is still too strong
for him, and sometimes before he even knows it,
he has throwed salvation away just grabbling
back at hoping. But it's all right—

STEVENS

You mean, when you have salvation, you dont
have hope?

NANCY

You dont even need it. All you need, all you
have to do, is just believe. So maybe—

STEVENS

Believe what?

NANCY

Just believe.—So maybe 'it's just as well that all
I did last night, was just to guess where you all
went. But I know now, and I know what the Big
Man told you. And it's all right. I finished all
that a long time back, that same day in the
judge's court. No: before that even: in the
nursery that night, before I even lifted my
hand—

TEMPLE

(convulsively)

Hush. Hush.

NANCY

All right. I've hushed. Because it's all right. I
can get low for Jesus too. I can get low for Him
too.

TEMPLE

Hush! Hush! At least, dont blaspheme. But who
am I to challenge the language you talk about

Him in, when He Himself certainly cant challenge it, since that's the only language He arranged for you to learn?

NANCY

What's wrong with what I said? Jesus is a man too. He's got to be. Menfolks listens to somebody because of what he says. Women dont. They dont care what he said. They listens because of what he is.

TEMPLE

Then let Him talk to me. I can get low for Him too, if that's all He wants, demands, asks. I'll do anything He wants if He'll just tell me what to do. No: how to do it. I know what to do, what I must do, what I've got to do. But how? We— I thought that all I would have to do would be to come back and go to the Big Man and tell him that it wasn't you who killed my baby, but I did it eight years ago that day when I slipped out the back door of that train, and that would be all. But we were wrong. Then I—we thought that all it would be was, for me just to come back here and tell you you had to die; to come all the way two thousand miles from California, to sit up all night driving to Jackson and talking for an hour or two and then driving back, to tell you you had to die; not just to bring you

the news that you had to die, because any messenger could do that, but just so it could be me
that would have to sit up all night and talk for
the hour or two hours and then bring you the
news back. You know: not to save you, that
wasn't really concerned in it: but just for me,
just for the suffering and the paying: a little
more suffering simply because there was a little
more time left for a little more of it, and we
might as well use it since we were already paying for it; and that would be all; it would be
finished then. But we were wrong again. That
was all, only for you. You wouldn't be any
worse off if I had never come back from California. You wouldn't even be any worse off.
And this time tomorrow, you wont be anything
at all. But not me. Because there's tomorrow,
and tomorrow, and tomorrow. All you've got to
do is, just to die. But let Him tell me what to do.
No: that's wrong; I know what to do, what I'm
going to do; I found that out that same night in
the nursery too. But let Him tell me how. How?
Tomorrow, and tomorrow, and still tomorrow.
How?

NANCY

Trust in Him.

TEMPLE

Trust in Him. Look what He has already done
to me. Which is all right; maybe I deserved it;
at least I'm not the one to criticise or dictate to
Him. But look what He did to you. Yet you can
still say that. Why? Why? Is it because there
isn't any thing else?

NANCY

I dont know. But you got to trust Him. Maybe
that's your pay for the suffering.

STEVENS

Whose suffering, and whose pay? Just each one's
for his own?

NANCY

Everybody's. All suffering. All poor sinning
man's.

STEVENS

The salvation of the world is in man's suffering.
Is that it?

NANCY

Yes, sir.

STEVENS

How?

NANCY

I dont know. Maybe when folks are suffering, they will be too busy to get into devilment, wont have time to worry and meddle one another.

TEMPLE

But why must it be suffering? He's omnipotent, or so they tell us. Why couldn't He have invented something else? Or, if it's got to be suffering, why cant it be just your own? Why cant you buy back your own sins with your own agony? Why do you and my little baby both have to suffer just because I decided to go to a baseball game eight years ago? Do you have to suffer everybody else's anguish just to believe in God? What kind of God is it that has to blackmail His customers with the whole world's grief and ruin?

NANCY

He dont want you to suffer. He dont like suffering neither. But He cant help Himself. He's like a man that's got too many mules. All of a sudden one morning, he looks around and sees more mules than he can count at one time even, let alone find work for, and all he knows is that they are his, because at least dont nobody else want to claim them, and that the pasture fence was still holding them last night where they

278 | REQUIEM FOR A NUN

cant harm themselves nor nobody else the least possible. And that when Monday morning comes, he can walk in there and hem some of them up and even catch them if he's careful about not never turning his back on the ones he aint hemmed up. And that, once the gear is on them, they will do his work and do it good, only he's still got to be careful about getting too close to them, or forgetting that another one of them is behind him, even when he is feeding them. Even when it's Saturday noon again, and he is turning them back into the pasture, where even a mule can know it's got until Monday morning anyway to run free in mule sin and mule pleasure.

STEVENS

You have got to sin, too?

NANCY

You aint *got* to. You cant help it. And He knows that. But you can suffer. And He knows that too. He dont tell you not to sin, He just asks you not to. And He dont tell you to suffer. But He gives you the chance. He gives you the best He can think of, that you are capable of doing. And He will save you.

STEVENS

You too? A murderess? In heaven?

NANCY

I can work.

STEVENS

The harp, the raiment, the singing, may not be for Nancy Mannigoe—not now. But there's still the work to be done—the washing and sweeping, maybe even the children to be tended and fed and kept from hurt and harm and out from under the grown folks' feet?

> (he pauses a moment. Nancy says nothing, immobile, looking at no one)

Maybe even that baby?

> (Nancy doesn't move, stir, not looking at anything apparently, her face still, bemused, expressionless)

That one too, Nancy? Because you loved that baby, even at the very moment when you raised your hand against it, knew that there was nothing left but to raise your hand?

> (Nancy doesn't answer nor stir)

A heaven where that little child will remember nothing of your hands but gentleness because now this earth will have been nothing but a dream that didn't matter? Is that it?

TEMPLE

Or maybe not that baby, not mine, because, since I destroyed mine myself when I slipped out the back end of that train that day eight years ago, I will need about all the forgiving and forgetting that one six-months-old baby is capable of. But the other one: yours: that you told me about, that you were carrying six months gone, and you went to the picnic or dance or frolic or fight or whatever it was, and the man kicked you in the stomach and you lost it? That one too?

STEVENS

(to Nancy)

What? Its father kicked you in the stomach while you were pregnant?

NANCY

I dont know.

STEVENS

You dont know who kicked you?

NANCY

I know that. I thought you meant its pa.

STEVENS

You mean, the man who kicked you wasn't even its father?

NANCY

I dont know. Any of them might have been.

STEVENS

Any of them? You dont have any idea who its father was?

NANCY

(looks at Stevens impatiently)

If you backed your behind into a buzz-saw, could you tell which tooth hit you first?

(to Temple)

What about that one?

TEMPLE

Will that one be there too, that never had a father and never was even born, to forgive you? Is there a heaven for it to go to so it can forgive you? Is there a heaven, Nancy?

NANCY

I dont know. I believes.

TEMPLE

Believe what?

NANCY

I dont know. But I believes.

They all pause at the sound of feet approaching beyond the exit door, all are looking at the door as the key

clashes again in the lock and the door swings out and
the Jailor enters, drawing the door to behind him.

JAILOR

(locking the door)

Thirty minutes, Lawyer. You named it, you
know: not me.

STEVENS

I'll come back later.

JAILOR

(turns and crosses toward
them)

Provided you dont put it off too late. What I
mean, if you wait until tonight to come back,
you might have some company; and if you put
it off until tomorrow, you wont have no client.

(to Nancy)

I found that preacher you want. He'll be here
about sundown, he said. He sounds like he might
even be another good baritone. And you cant
have too many, especially as after tonight you
wont need none, huh? No hard feelings, Nancy.
You committed about as horrible a crime as this
county ever seen, but you're fixing to pay the law
for it, and if the child's own mother—

(he falters, almost pauses,
catches himself and continues briskly, moving again)

There, talking too much again. Come on, if Lawyer's through with you. You can start taking your time at daylight tomorrow morning, because you might have a long hard trip.

He passes her and goes briskly on toward the alcove at rear. Nancy turns to follow.

> **TEMPLE**
> (quickly)

Nancy.

> (Nancy doesn't pause. Temple continues, rapidly)

What about me? Even if there is one and somebody waiting in it to forgive me, there's still tomorrow and tomorrow. And suppose tomorrow and tomorrow, and then nobody there, nobody waiting to forgive me—

> **NANCY**
> (moving on after the Jailor)

Believe.

> **TEMPLE**

Believe what, Nancy? Tell me.

> **NANCY**

Believe.

She exits into the alcove behind the Jailor. The steel door off-stage clangs, the key clashes. Then the Jailor reappears, approaches, and crosses toward the exit. He unlocks the door and opens it out again, pauses.

JAILOR

Yes, sir. A long hard way. If I was ever fool enough to commit a killing that would get my neck into a noose, the last thing I would want to see would be a preacher. I'd a heap rather believe there wasn't nothing after death than to risk the station where I was probably going to get off.

> (he waits, holding the door, looking back at them. Temple stands motionless until Stevens touches her arm slightly. Then she moves, stumbles slightly and infinitesimally, so infinitesimally and so quickly recovered that the Jailor has barely time to react to it, though he does so: with quick concern, with that quality about him almost gentle, almost articulate, turning from the door, even leaving it open as he starts quickly toward her)

Here; you set down on the bench; I'll get you a glass of water.

> (to Stevens)

Durn it, Lawyer, why did you have to bring her—

TEMPLE
> (recovered)

I'm all right.

She walks steadily toward the door. The Jailor watches her.

JAILOR

You sure?

TEMPLE
> (walking steadily and rapidly toward him and the door now)

Yes. Sure.

JAILOR
> (turning back toward the door)

Okay. I sure dont blame you. Durned if I see how even a murdering nigger can stand this smell.

He passes on out the door and exits, invisible though still holding the door and waiting to lock it.

Temple, followed by Stevens, approaches the door.

JAILOR'S VOICE
(off-stage: surprised)
Howdy. Gowan, here's your wife now.

TEMPLE
(walking)
Anyone to save it. Anyone who wants it. If there
is none, I'm sunk. We all are. Doomed. Damned.

STEVENS
(walking)
Of course we are. Hasn't He been telling us that
for going on two thousand years?

GOWAN'S VOICE
(off-stage)
Temple.

TEMPLE
Coming.

They exit. The door closes in, clashes, the clash and clang
of the key as the Jailor locks it again; the three pairs of
footsteps sound and begin to fade in the outer corridor.

Curtain